5,000

Designs and Motifs from India

Edited by

AJIT MOOKERJEE

DOVER PUBLICATIONS, INC.
Mineola, New York

Bibliographical Note

This Dover edition, first published in 1996, is an unabridged, slightly corrected republication of the work first published by The Indian Institute of Art in Industry: Artistry House, Calcutta, India, in 1958, under the title *5000 Indian Designs and Motifs*. The publisher is grateful to Duke University for making their copy of this book available for reprinting.

Library of Congress Cataloging-in-Publication Data

5000 designs and motifs from India
    5000 Indian designs and motifs edited by Ajit Mookerjee.
        p.   cm.
    Includes index.
    ISBN 0-486-29061-1 (pbk.)
    1. Decoration and ornament—India—Themes, motives.   I. Mookerjee, Ajit.   II. Title.
NK1476.A1A18   1996
745.4′49′54—dc20   96-11366
                                                                  CIP

Manufactured in the United States of America
Dover Publications, Inc., 31 East 2nd Street, Mineola, N.Y. 11501

FOREWORD

THE ILLUSTRATIONS presented in this book have been selected from different sources as typical of Indian traditional designs and motifs. In spite of their variety and complexity, an unerring thread of continuity, growing out of the inner logic and dynamism of the people from region to region, connects these elements. These designs and motifs may be a great source of inspiration to the designer-artist who can take full advantage of them. All such designs have a special Indian quality and the designer-artist should be at home with them—and through them, with the treasures of India. Our principal aim in presenting them in book form is to offer a glimpse into the rich store of Indian decorative art.

I wish to express my thanks to Mr. N. R. Gopalakrishnan and to Mr. Gouri Ghose for their cooperation and particularly to the three artists, Miss Arati Roy, Mr. Indu Bhusan Gupta and Mr. Sushil Das, for the copy work. I am also grateful to Dr. Verrier Elwin and the Oxford University Press for the permission to reproduce the tribal decorations in the last four plates of the book.

A. M.

NOTES

TRADITIONAL DESIGNS AND MOTIFS : 3000 B. C. TO MODERN TIMES

PLATES 1—5

Harappa culture: mainly Mohenjo-daro and Harappa seals, dolls and toys, pottery including Nal

PLATES 6—8

Sanchi Stupas: mainly railings and gateways

PLATES 9—15

Punch-marked coins and pottery: mainly Taxila and South India

PLATES 16—22

Ajanta and Bagh murals

PLATES 23—44

Muslim monuments: mainly Agra, Delhi, Sikandra, Fatehpur Sikri, Bijapur, Lahore, Jaunpur, etc.

PLATES 45—52

Buddhist, Jain and Brahminical temples

PLATES 53—105

Jewellery and metal wares: mainly Rajasthan, South India, including folk specimens

PLATES 106—152

Textiles: woven—mainly Banaras, Orissa, Dacca, Gujarat, Maharashtra; printed—mainly Jaipur, Murshidabad, South India, Gujarat; embroidered—mainly Punjab, Saurashtra, Himachal Pradesh, Hyderabad, Assam, Manipur, including Bengal Kanthas

PLATES 153—166

Paintings and drawings: mainly Orissa, Bengal, Rajasthan including Alpana, Kolam and Kasoti

PLATES 167—195

Miscellaneous items including migration of Indian motifs

PLATES 196—200

Masks and tribal arts: mainly Orissa, Naga, Bengal and Madhya Pradesh

v

INTRODUCTION

ART IS applied life. India, which has had a rich and varied existence for thousands of years, has naturally come to inherit a unique art tradition. Indian art in its distinctive form is now increasingly being recognized as worthy of study and appreciation. Universal in character, it has at the same time its own well-defined features, influencing, and being influenced by, other forms of art.

Indian decorative art as a special subject of study has not yet been taken up seriously although random references to it in many of the books and treatises on the broader subject of Indian art have served to invite more attention to it. Decoration is part of any object of art and as such is discussed often along with its integral quality. A separate study of this area is warranted because of its adaptability for modern application. Modern designing in India is a recent trend and, with a growing appreciation of its values, designers are apt to look back to traditional forms and to contemporary developments for their inspiration and sustenance with equal measure. To help such designers (and others interested in the subject) this modest publication is attempted.

In application of designs, the artists of old seldom lost their sense of proportion and balance and the main theme of the work was never lost sight of in the exuberance of decoration. Degeneration followed as a later phenomenon.

Indian art in general, no doubt, provides adequate material for the study of decorative arts. But it is in the actual articles of daily use or other ancillary objects that the designs and motifs are so well preserved and handed down from generation to generation. A study of Indian art from a purely aesthetic point of view will reveal that over a wide field, in the artistic sensibility of the people, there is a surprising continuity from one epoch to another. The basic continuity is not achieved at the sacrifice of flexibility of forms and designs. On the other hand, the popular standard of taste has been maintained throughout because of the scope for such transformation and change. This continuity is, however, not like that of a stagnant pool. So long as the craftsman functioned and he set his personal seal on the things he produced, there was no risk of any violent change in their appeal nor was there any sudden break with the past. Art was conditioned by the function of the craft object, which in turn guided the life movement of the people in any given surrounding. In other words, decoration was a part of the function; it grew from within and was seldom imposed externally. Artistic skill was not acquired, but inborn; art and life went hand in hand for they were never thought of separately. As life was conditioned by religion, customs and codes, so too were arts and crafts. Conflict could not arise because an alternative social structure did not present itself until the industrial age. The revolutionary change brought about by industrialization could not be an easy one. Old values crumbled and, because no new values could be readily found, there was the inevitable sense of frustration. When the craftsman of old disappeared the standards set by him vanished with him. Yet the machine which took his place failed to guide popular sensibility or to produce any aesthetic standard. In the place of the quality products by the craftsman, the machine took charge and substituted quantity. Where the one excelled in individuality and personal touch, the other went by sheer number and anonymity. When production on a large scale became possible by the use of the machine, the products were characterless.

The craftsman who inherited the "group soul" or the sum total of artistic consciousness preceding him, functioned at his best when both his material and spiritual satisfaction were assured by society. Coomaraswamy says, "It has only been when the craftsman has had the right to work, the right to work faithfully, a right to the due reward of his labour, and at the same time a conscious or subconscious faith in the social and spiritual significance of his work, that his art possessed the elements of real greatness." In the cataclysm that industrialization brought about, both these elements, so conducive to greatness in art and craft in the preceding ages, were lost to the craftsman. As a factory hand, his material condition worsened and, more than that, he lost the dignity and status which went unsolicited to him in a village economy.

Industrialization also meant a division of labour so complete yet up to the time quite unknown. The craftsman was both the designer and the manufacturer and was therefore free to set a standard for himself in his craft. Industrialization cut these two into a number of different compartments and, in any event, the craftsman played an insignificant role in a complicated process. Moreover, as the designer and the manufacturer combined in the traditional craftsman, he could command the shape, form, colour, etc. of the product.

The modern age may be incapable of recreating the past. The machine has entered so much in our life and it promises to be more emphatic in the days of the future. There is, on the other hand, the chance of evolving a new and abiding culture by the judicial integration of machine and handicraft. In the present context, "judicial integration" means instillation of a sense of design in the manufacturing process so that we recapture a little of that colour and form in the things of everyday use which were so characteristic in the days of the craftsman.

A mere copying of the past, however adept, will not help; for that past was conditioned by so many factors that have since vanished. Moreover, what will predominantly guide the design movement in the present and the future is science. The use of science in everyday life will grow at a faster rate than what we can imagine now. In any case, we have to take into account that science has already opened a new vista of possibilities by the invention of a number of synthetic materials, and the progress is continuing at a gathering speed. It is hoped that the underlying beauty of the thousands of designs and motifs offered here will serve the purpose of producing new shapes and patterns, expressive of the modern urge based on formulae of the old.

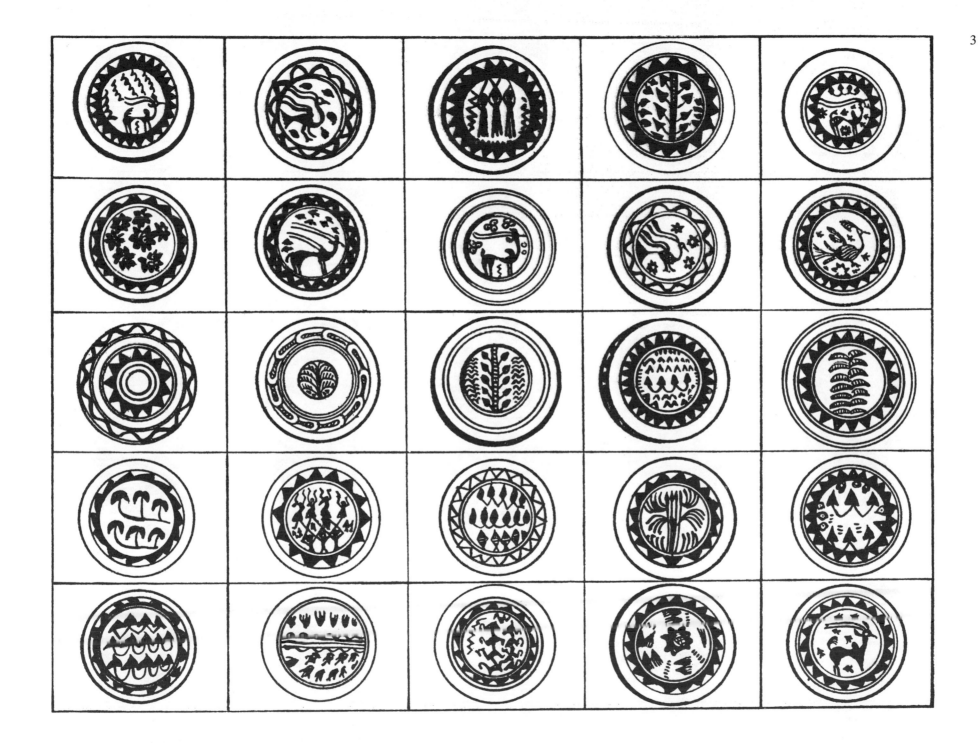

3

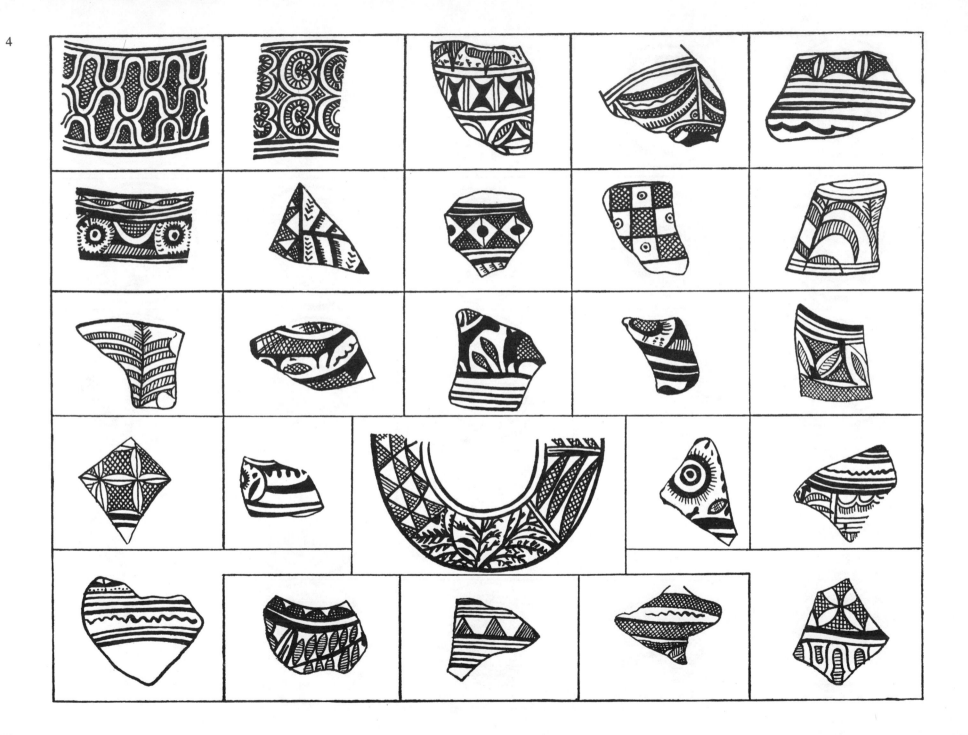

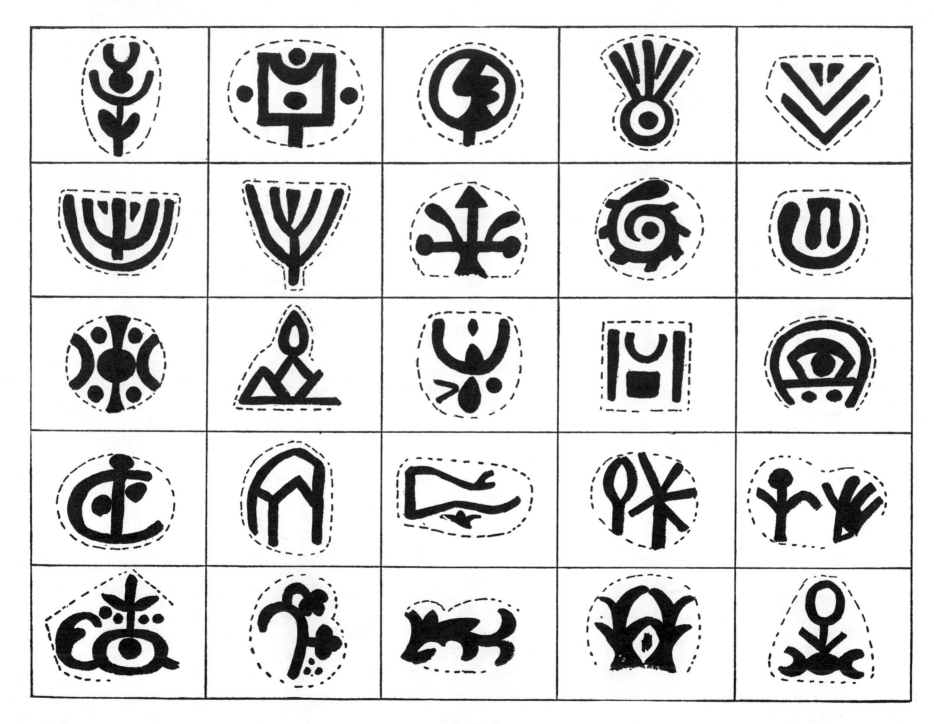

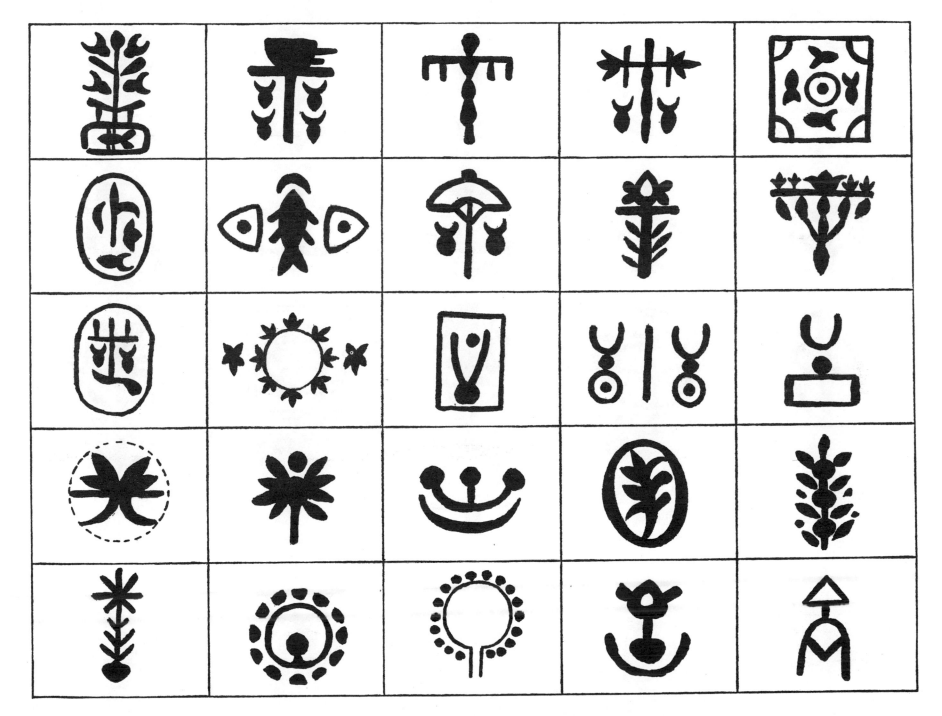

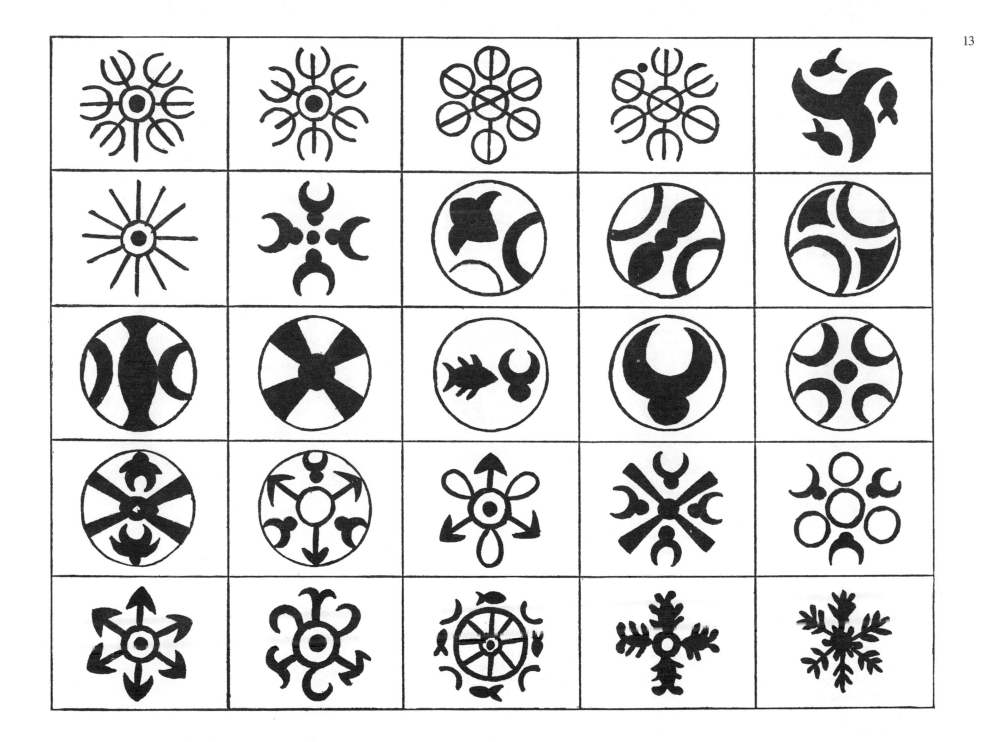

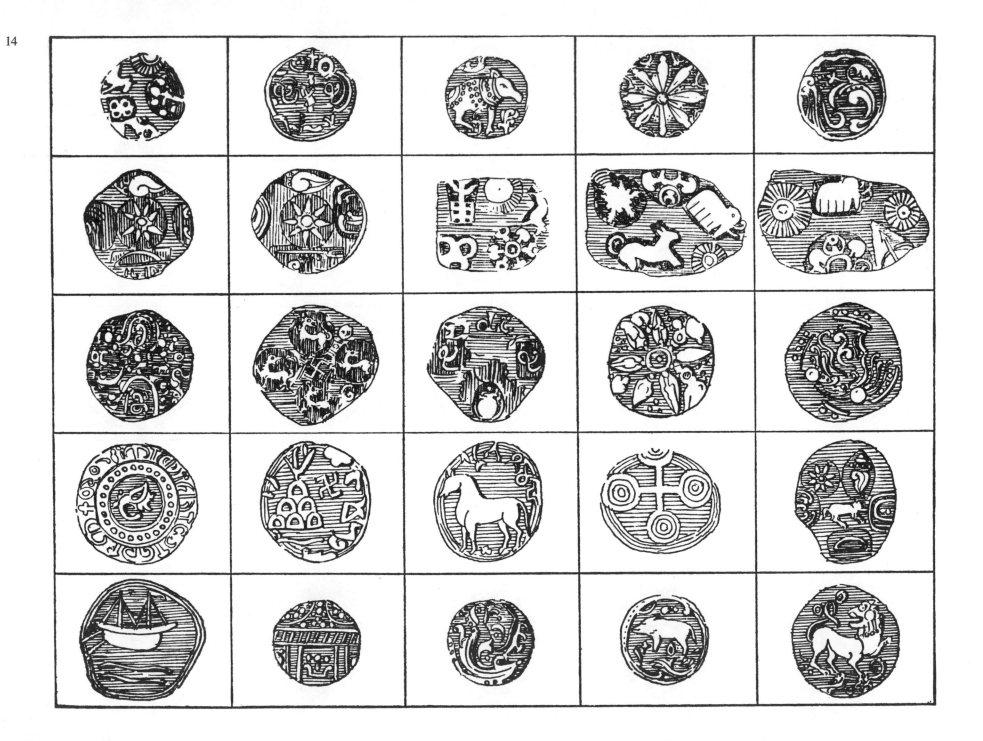

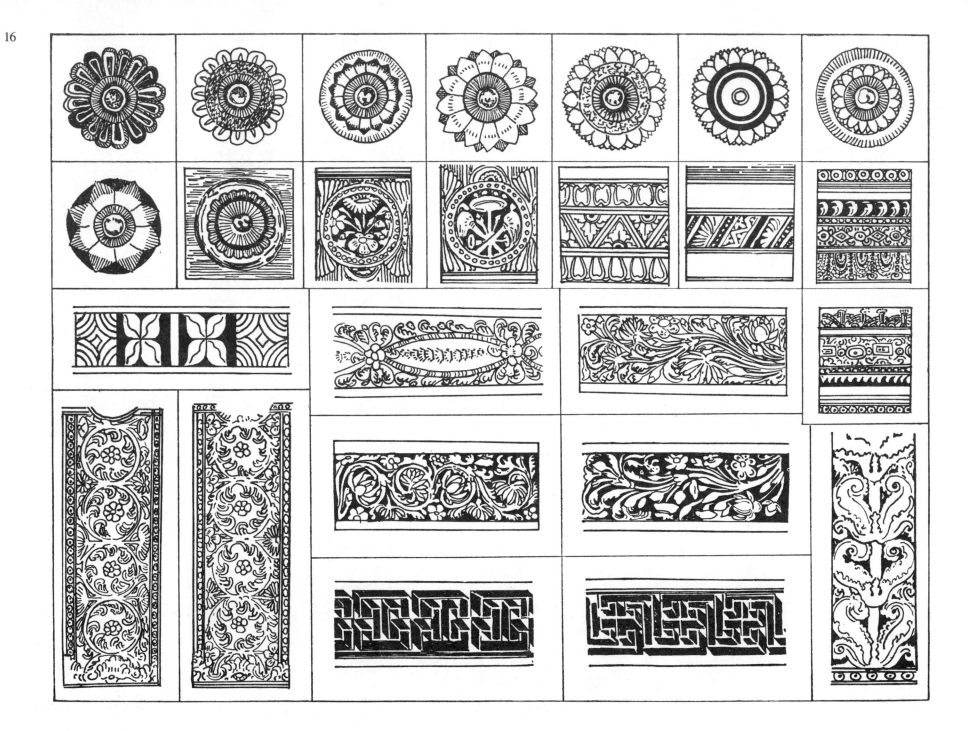

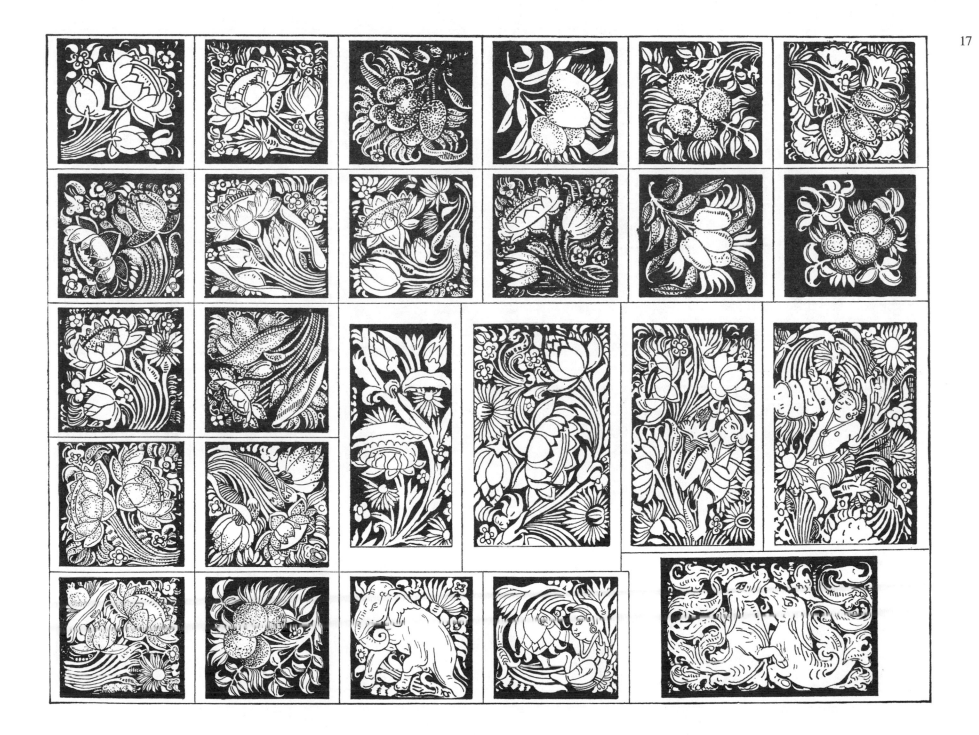

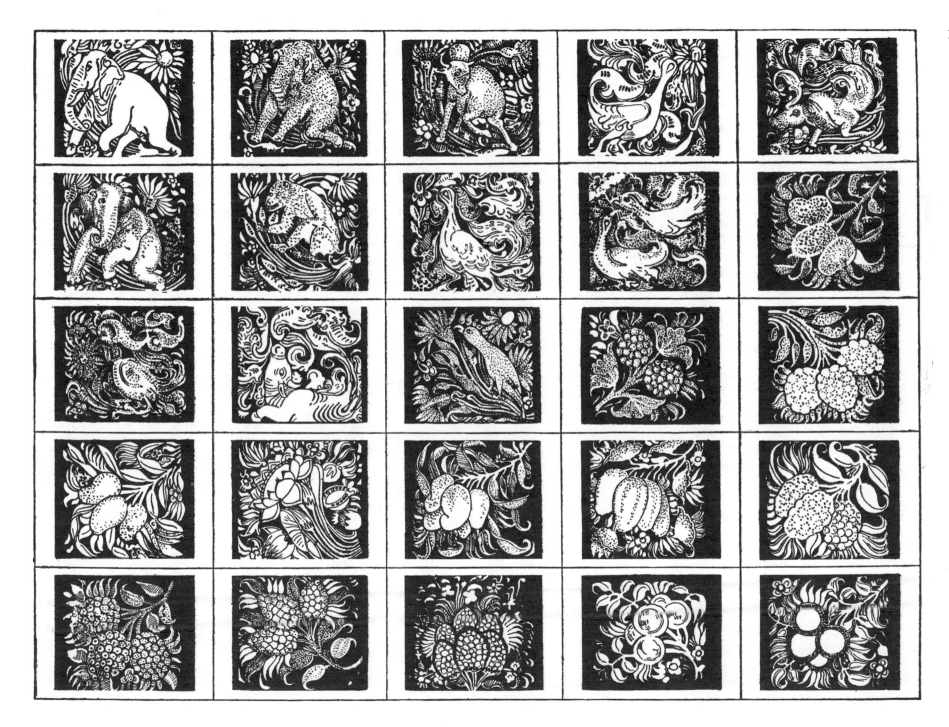

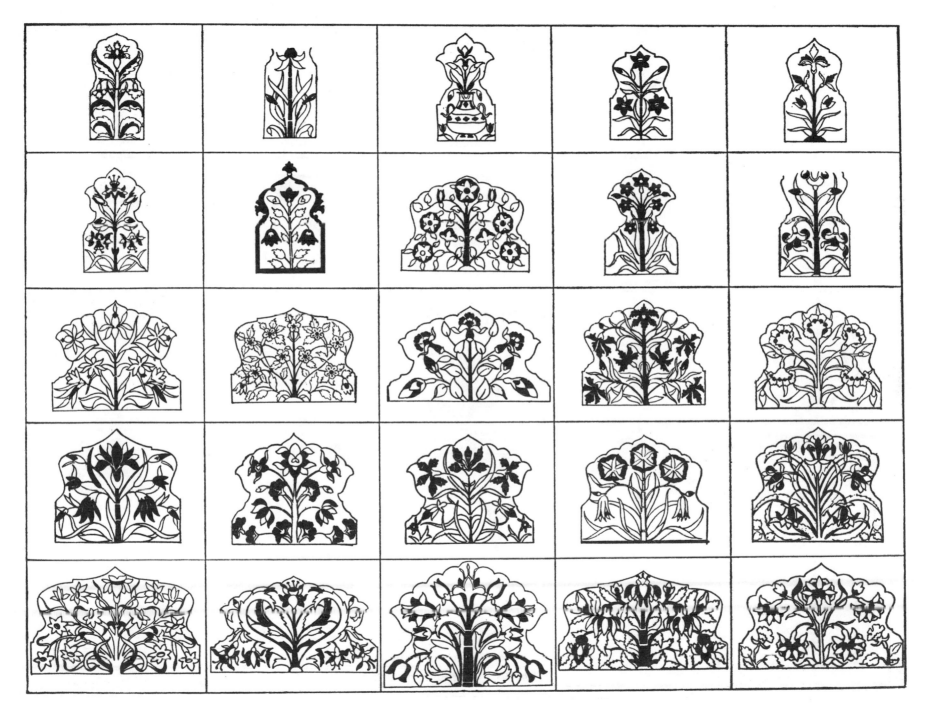

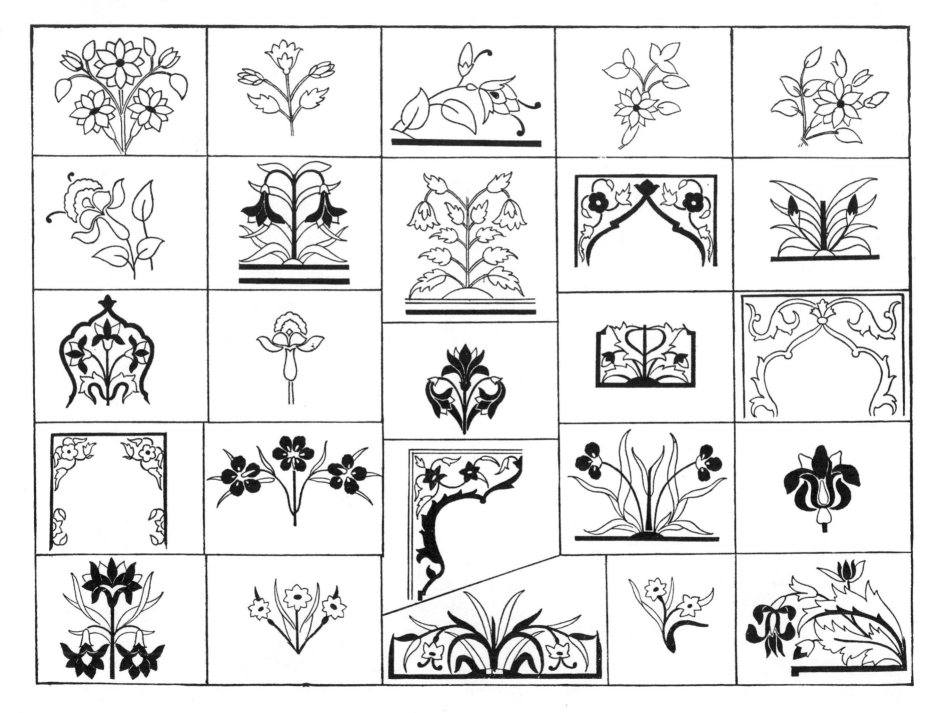

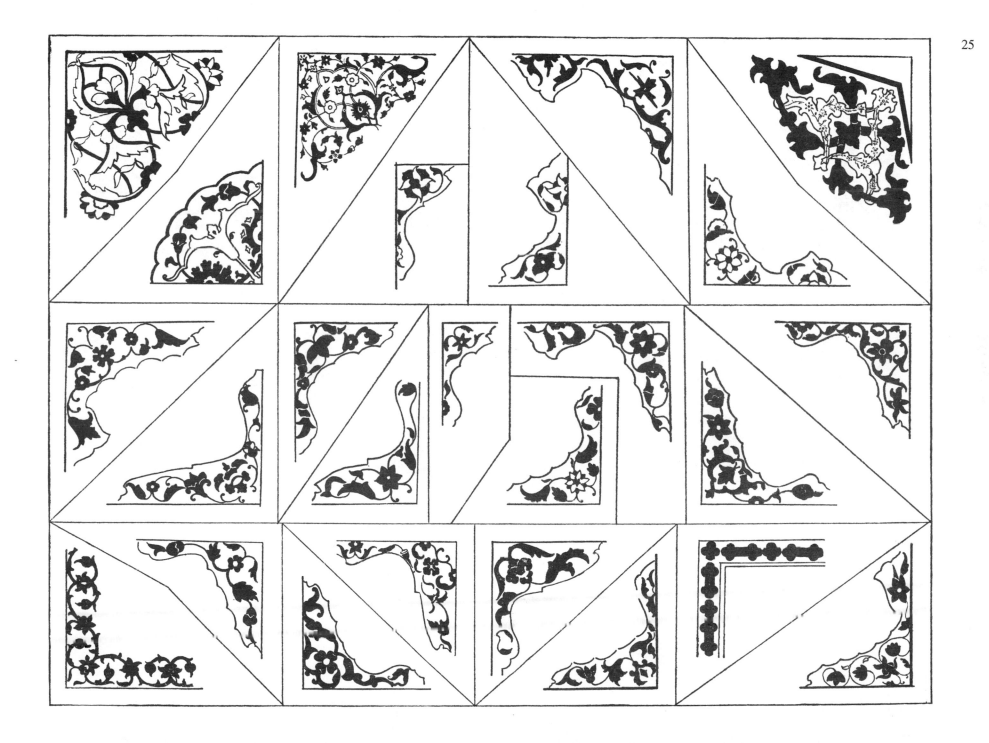

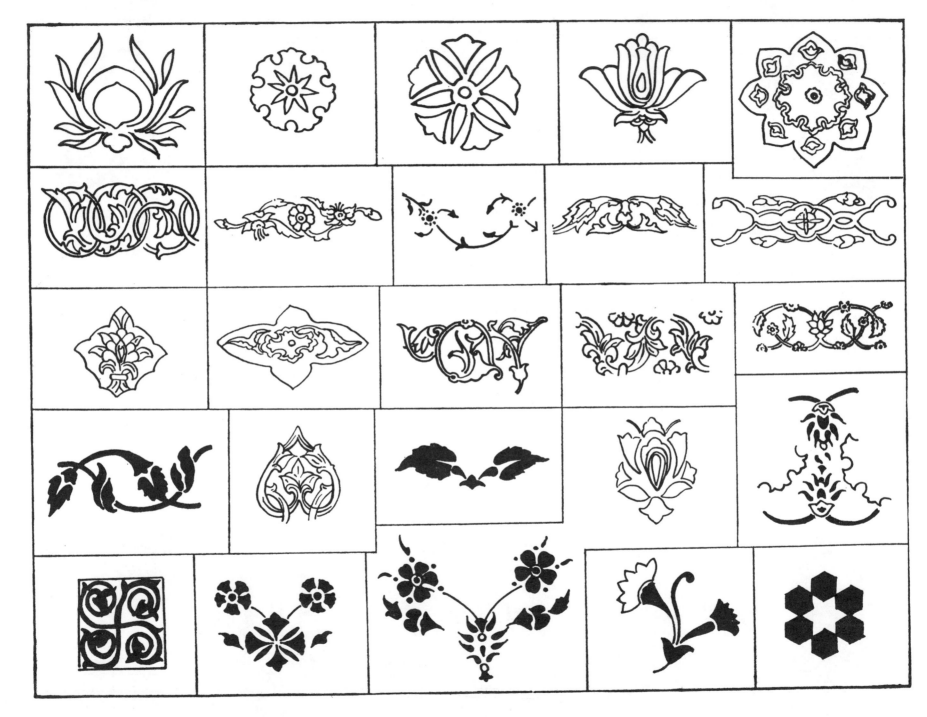

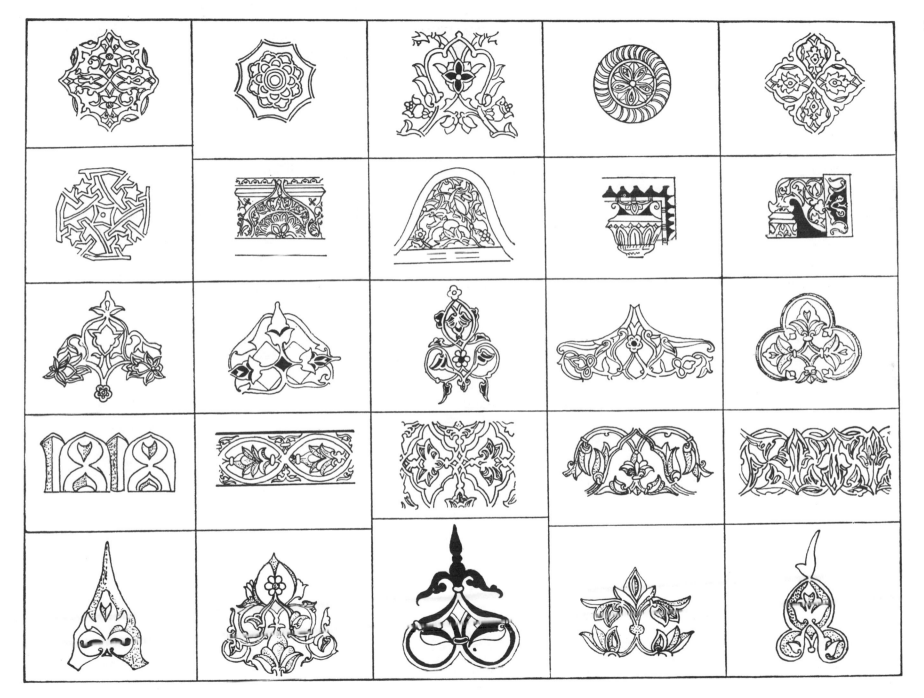

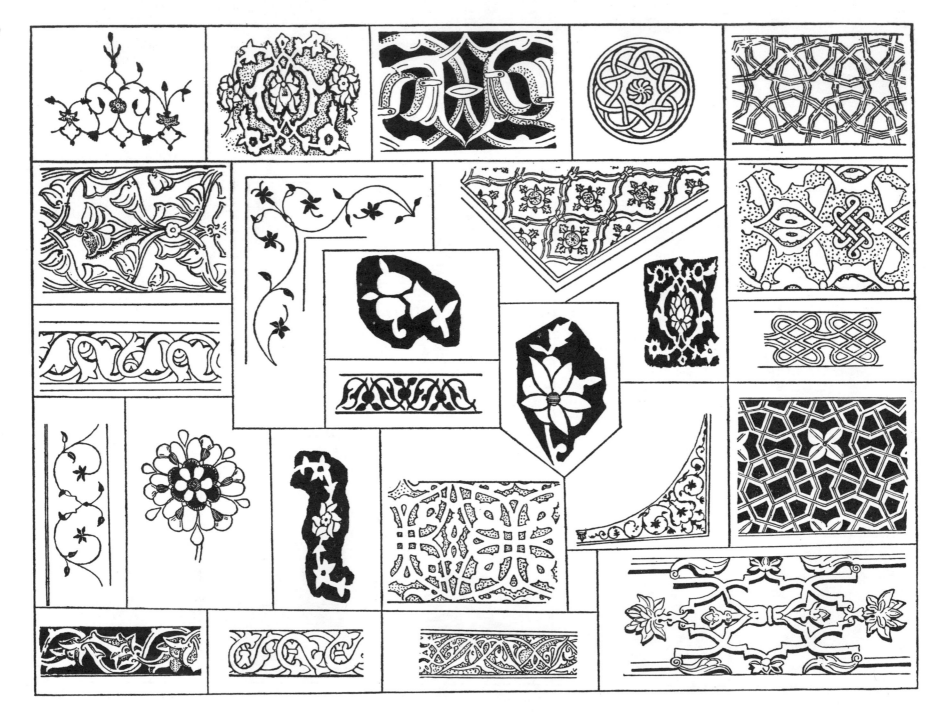

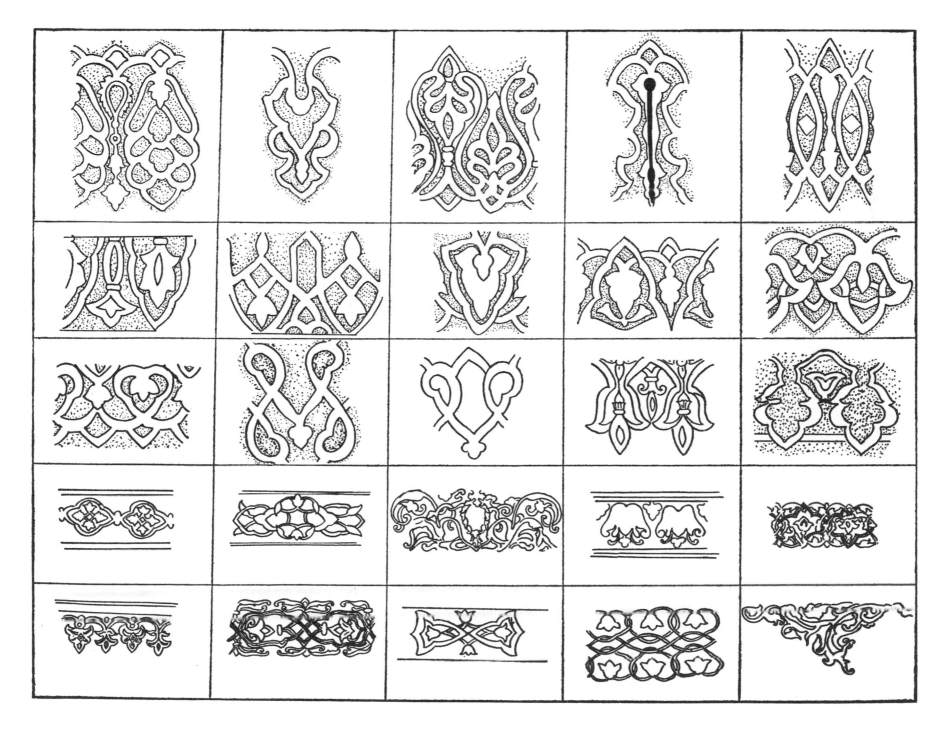

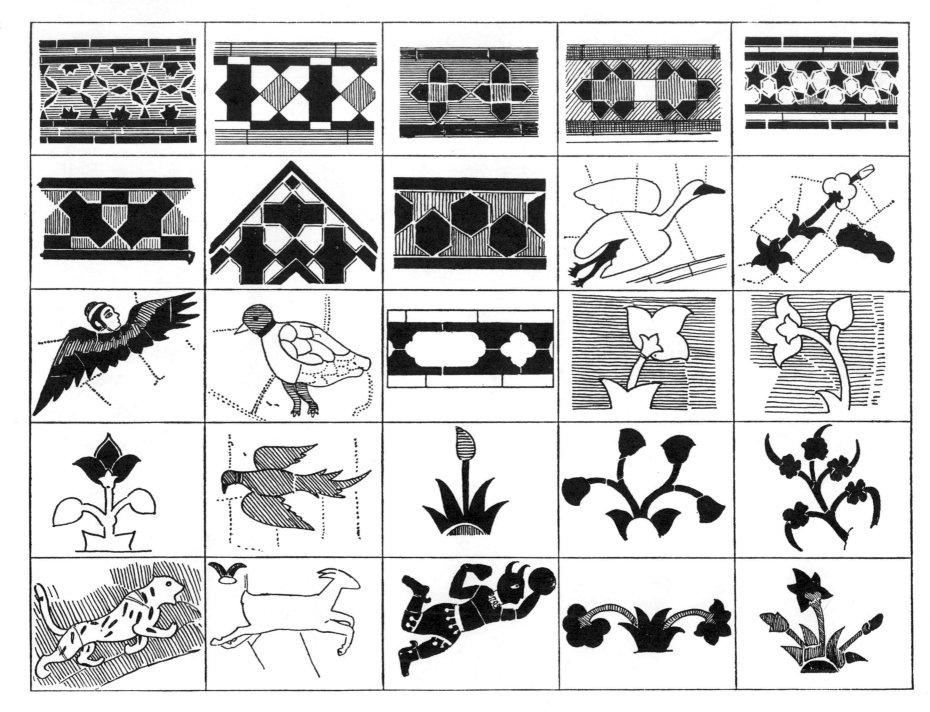

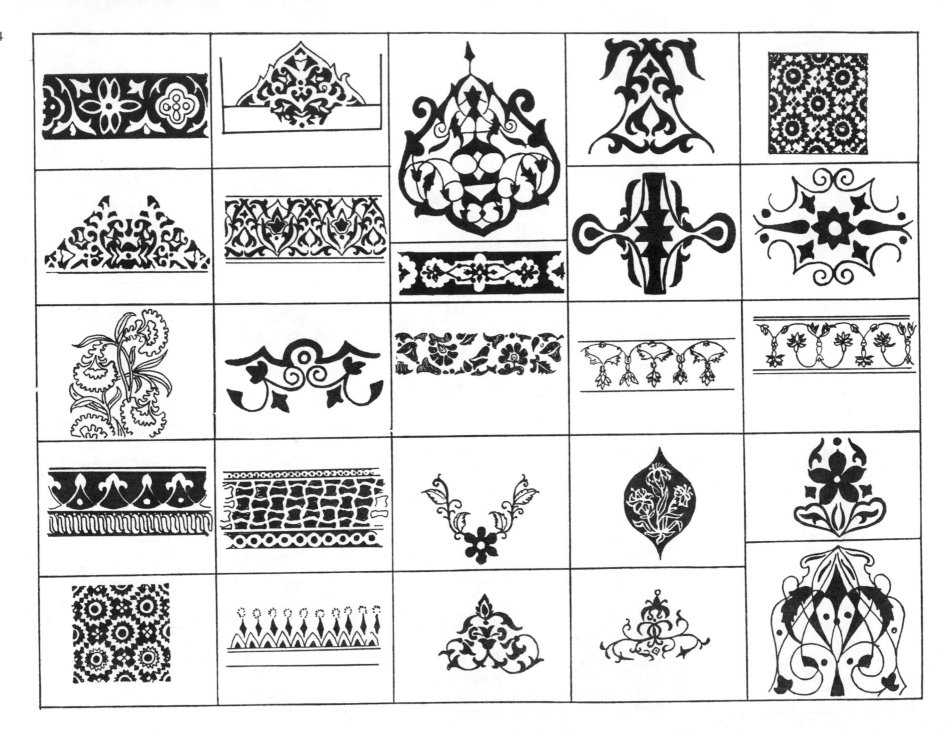

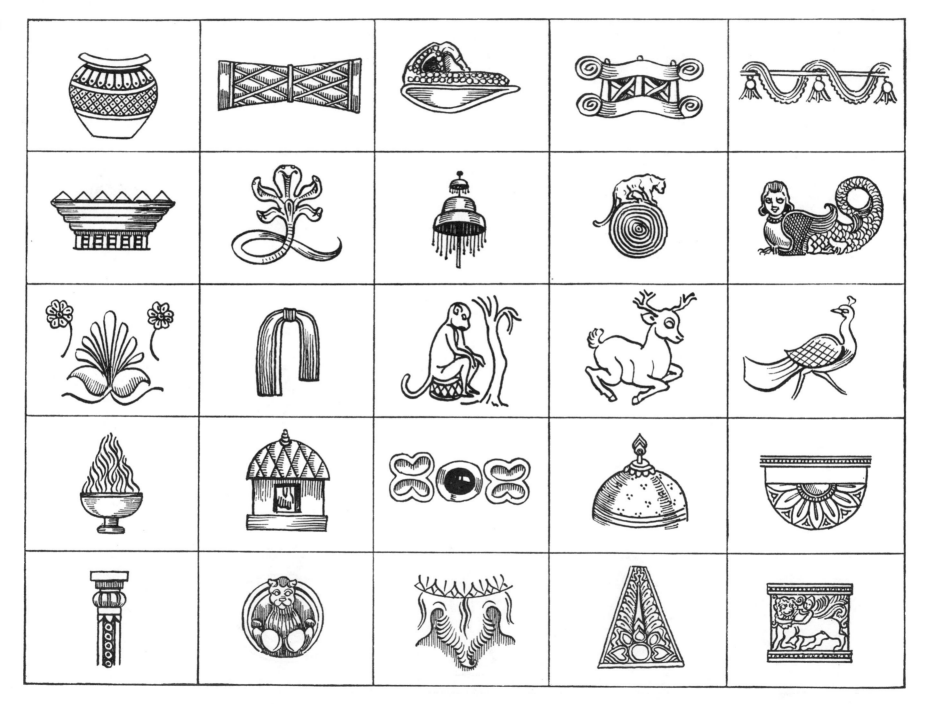

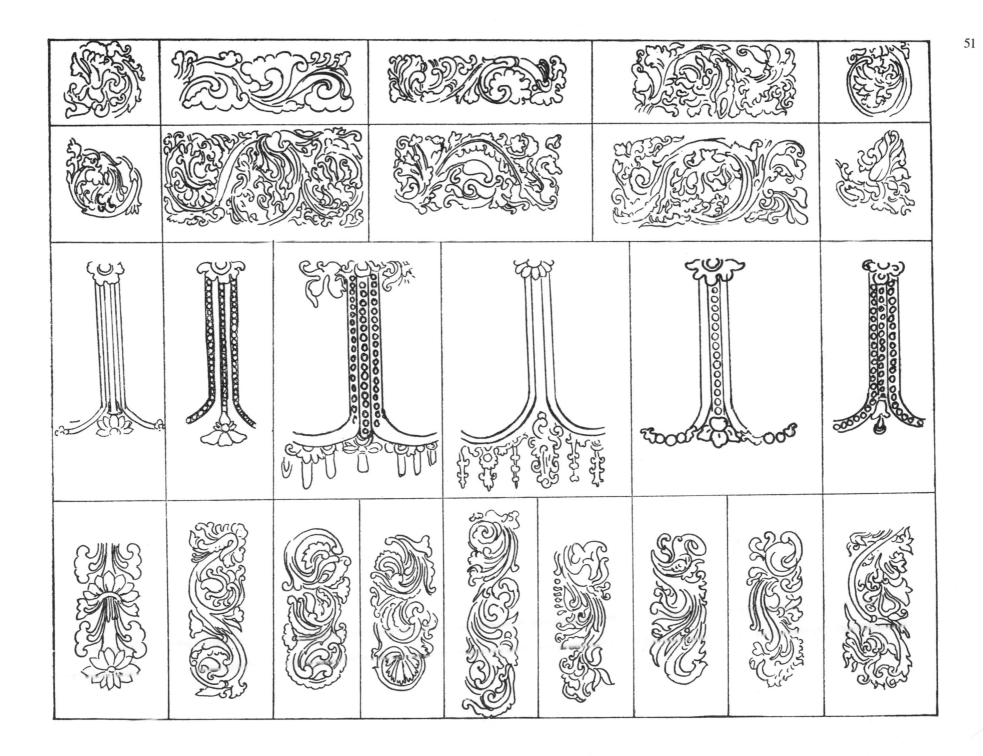

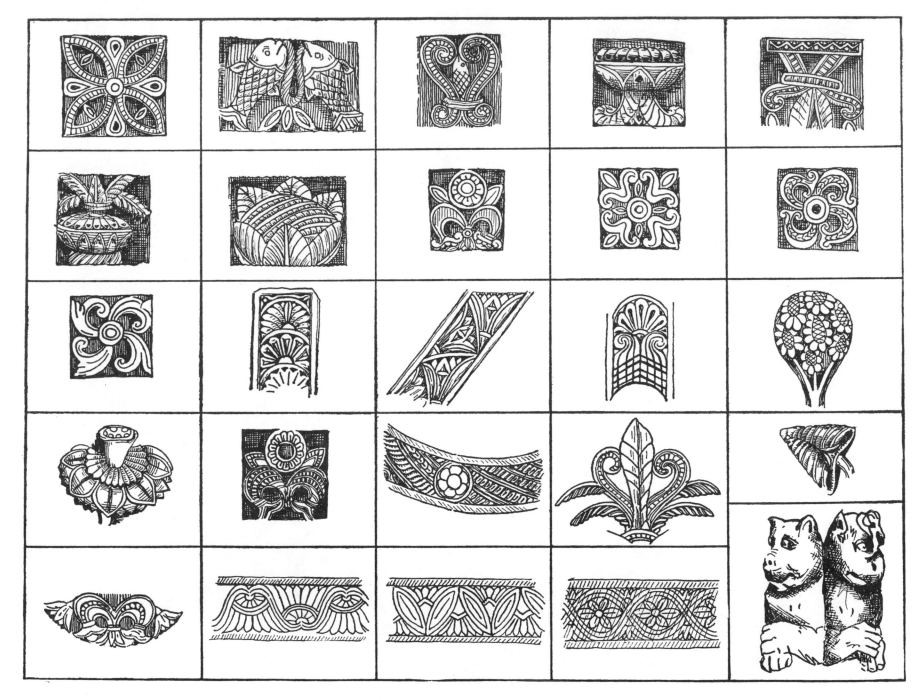

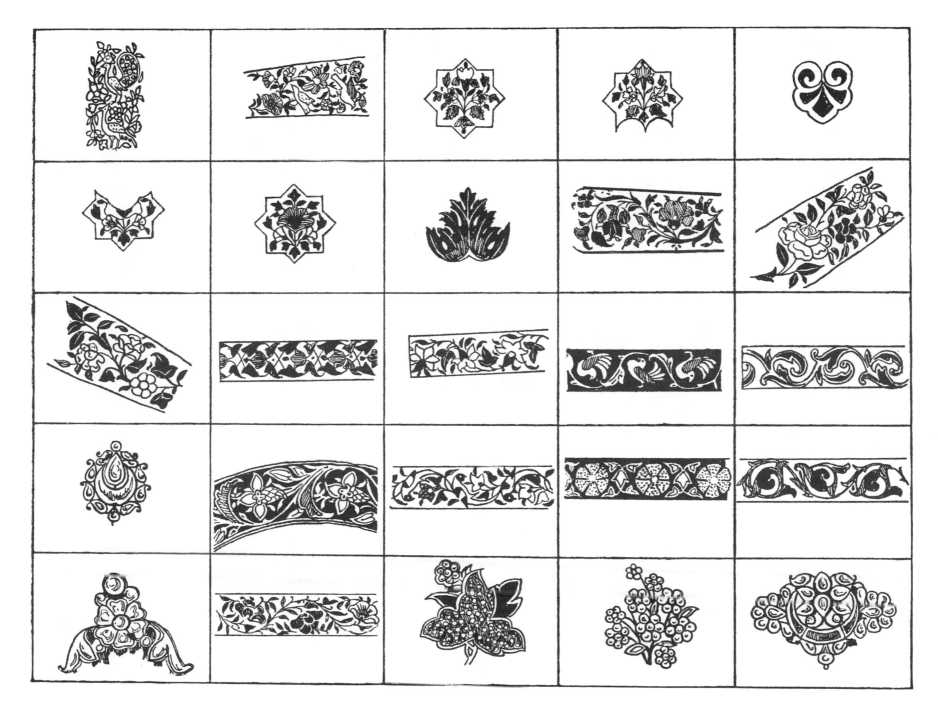

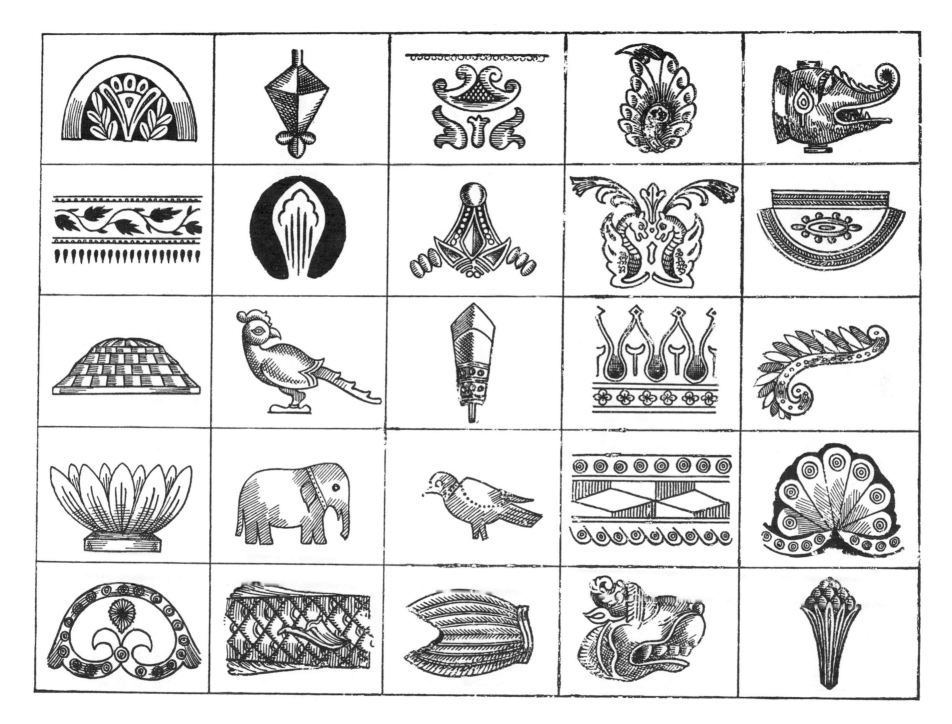

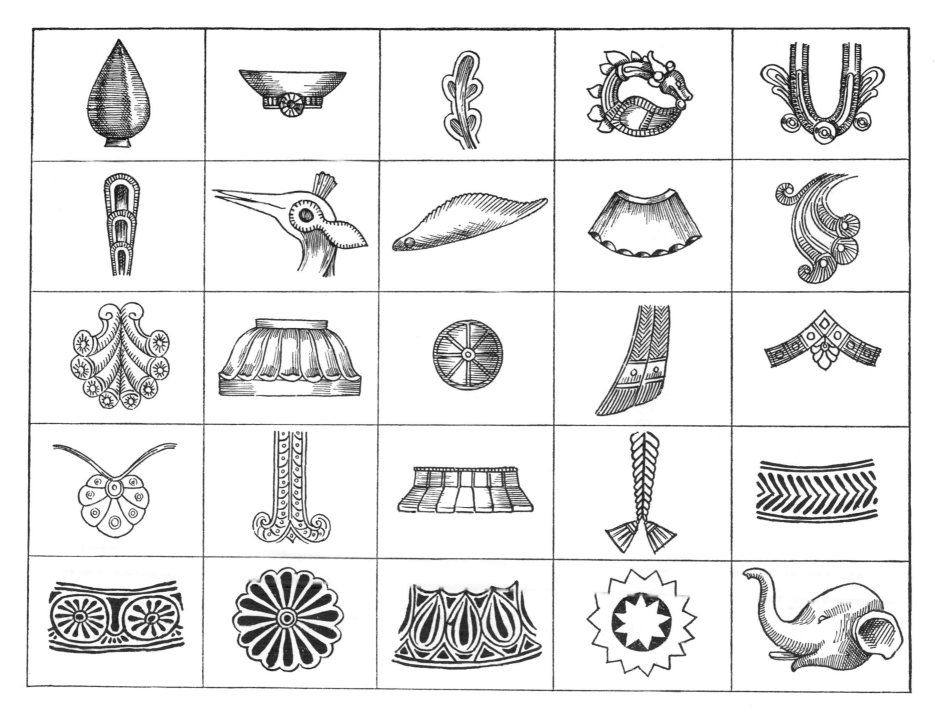

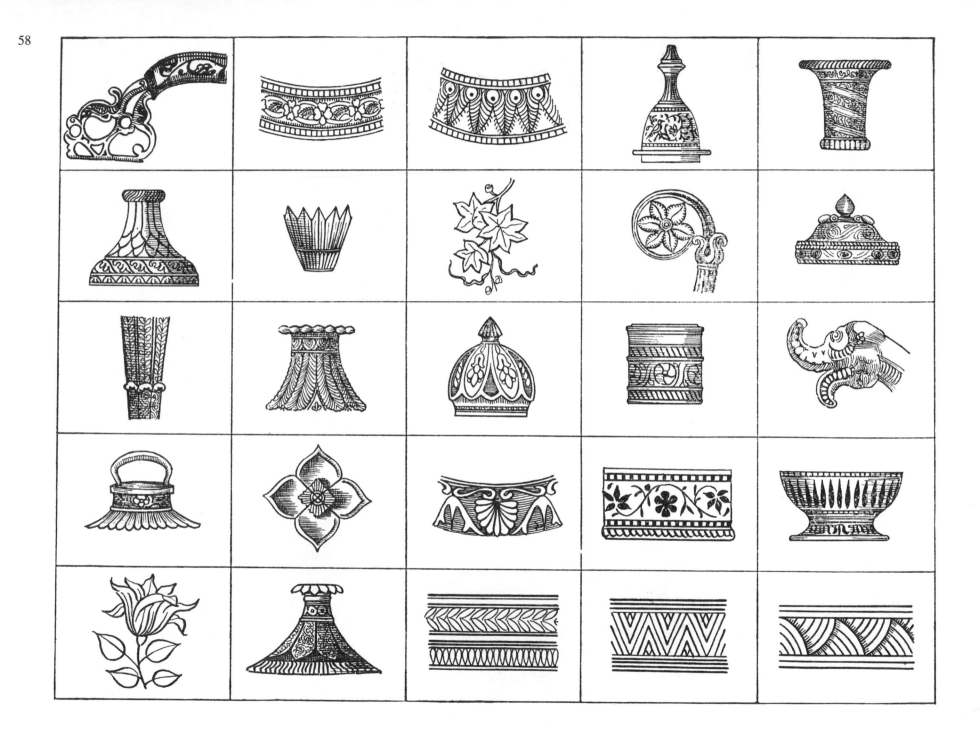

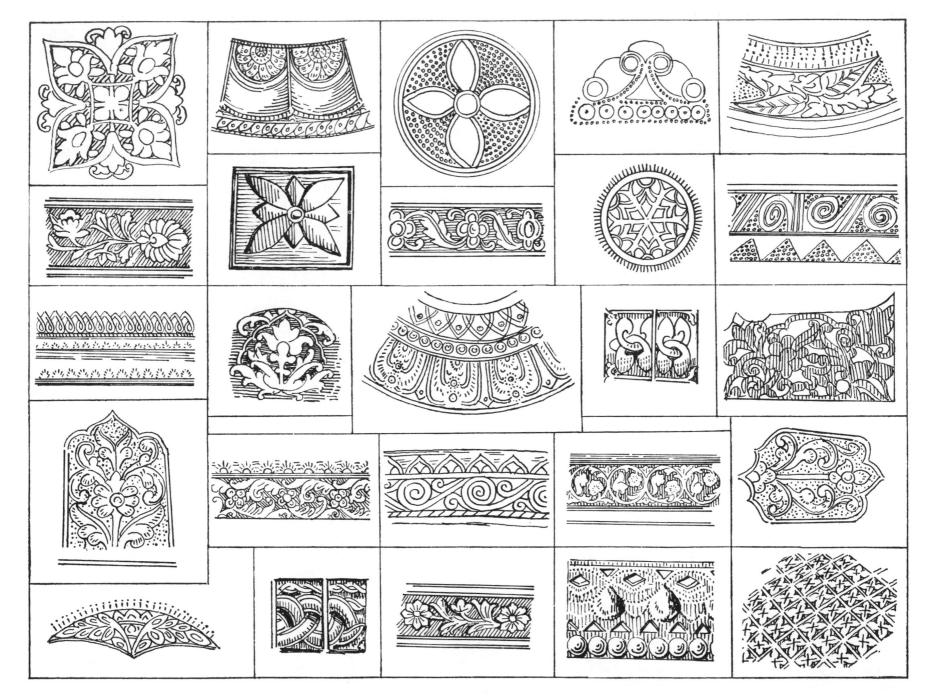

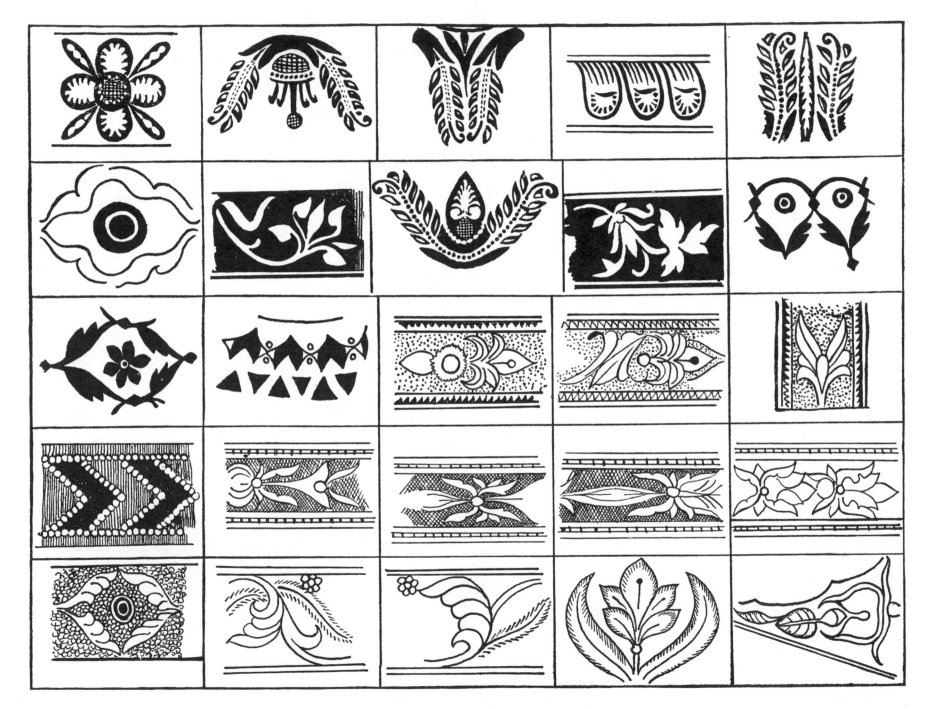

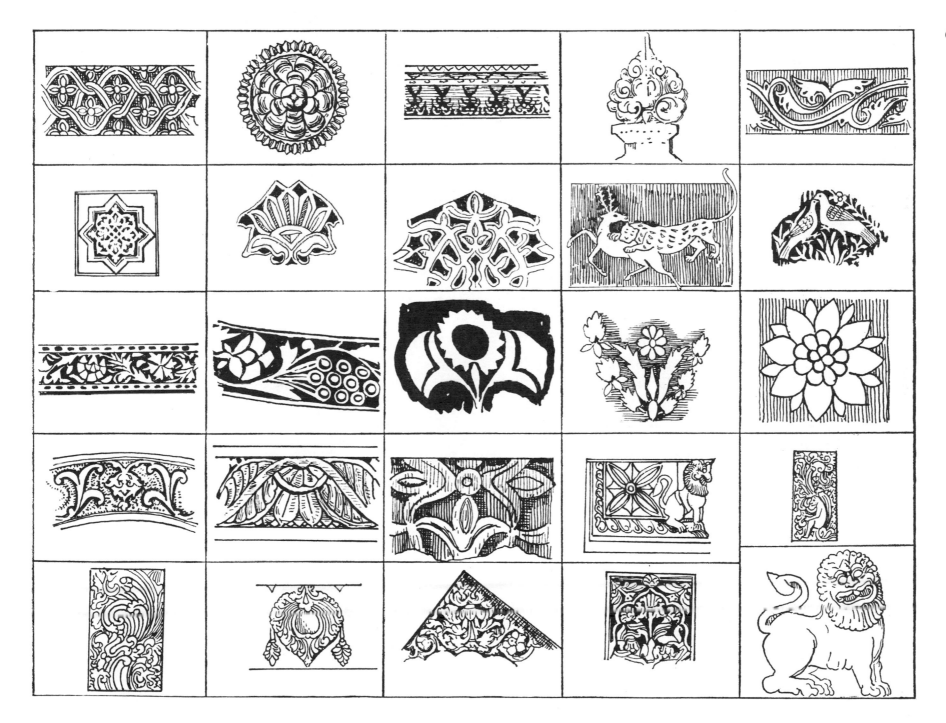

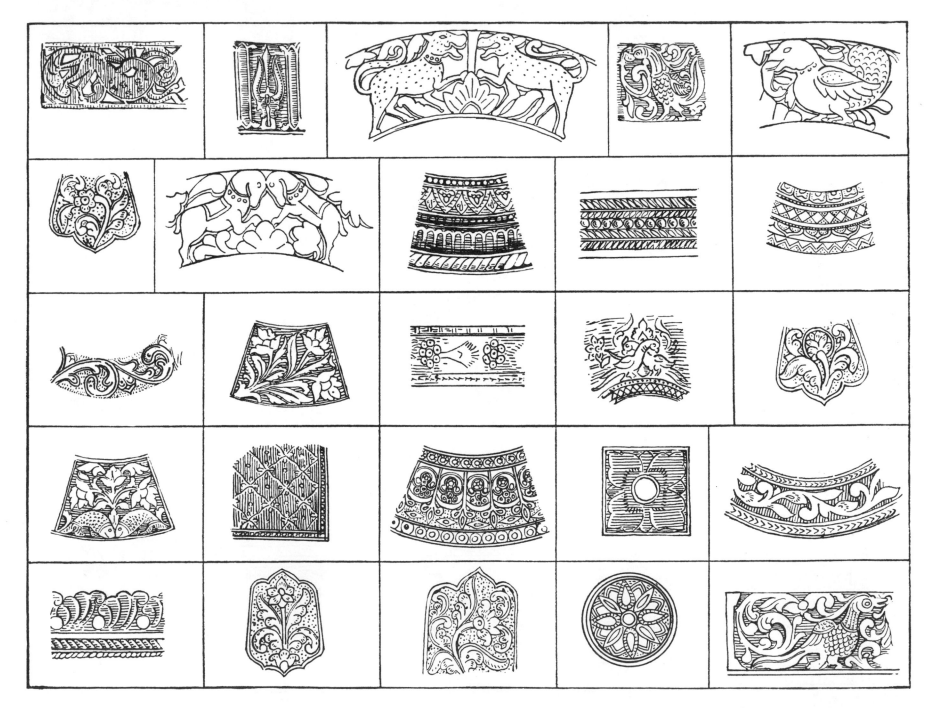

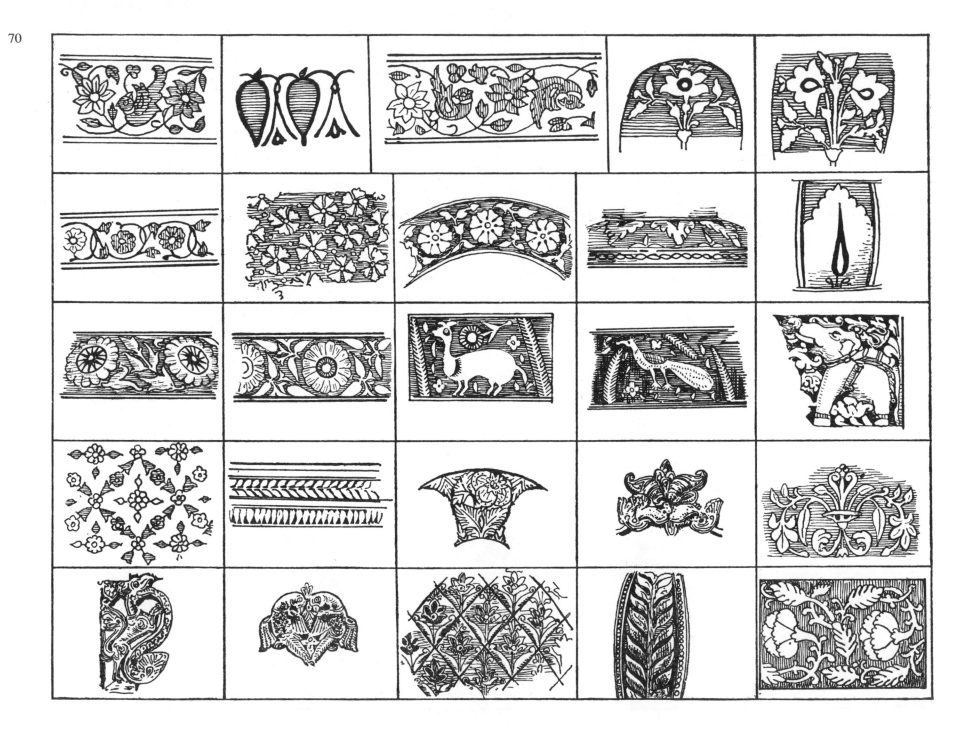

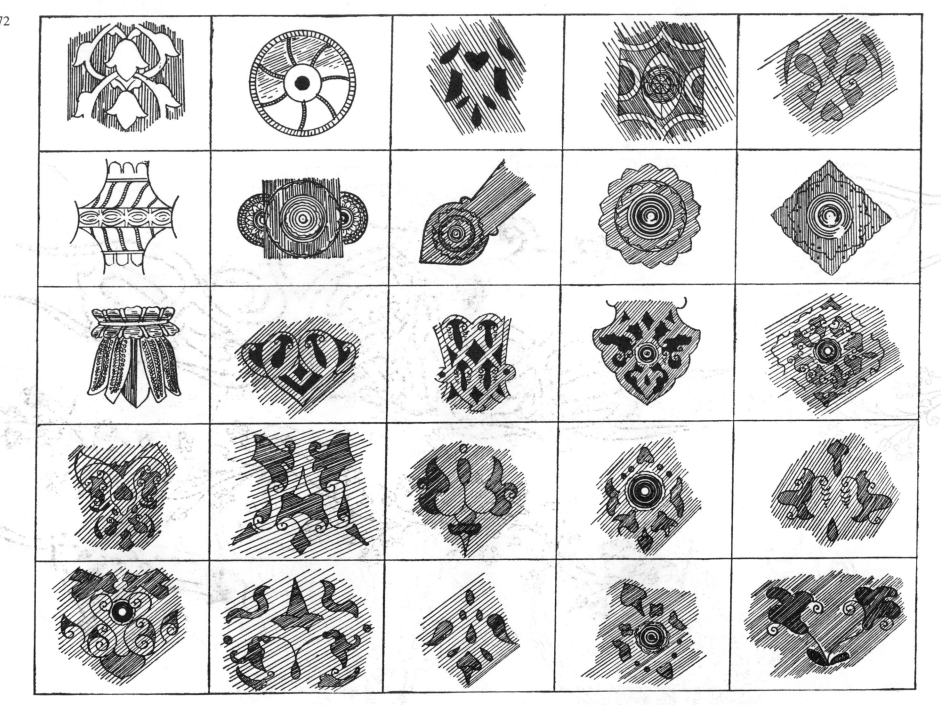

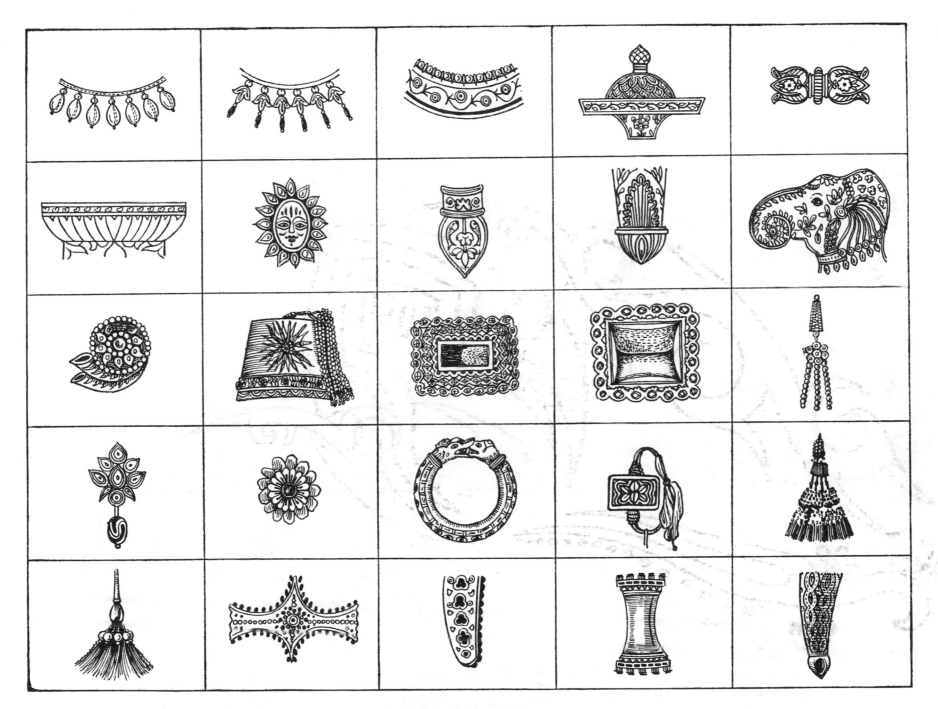

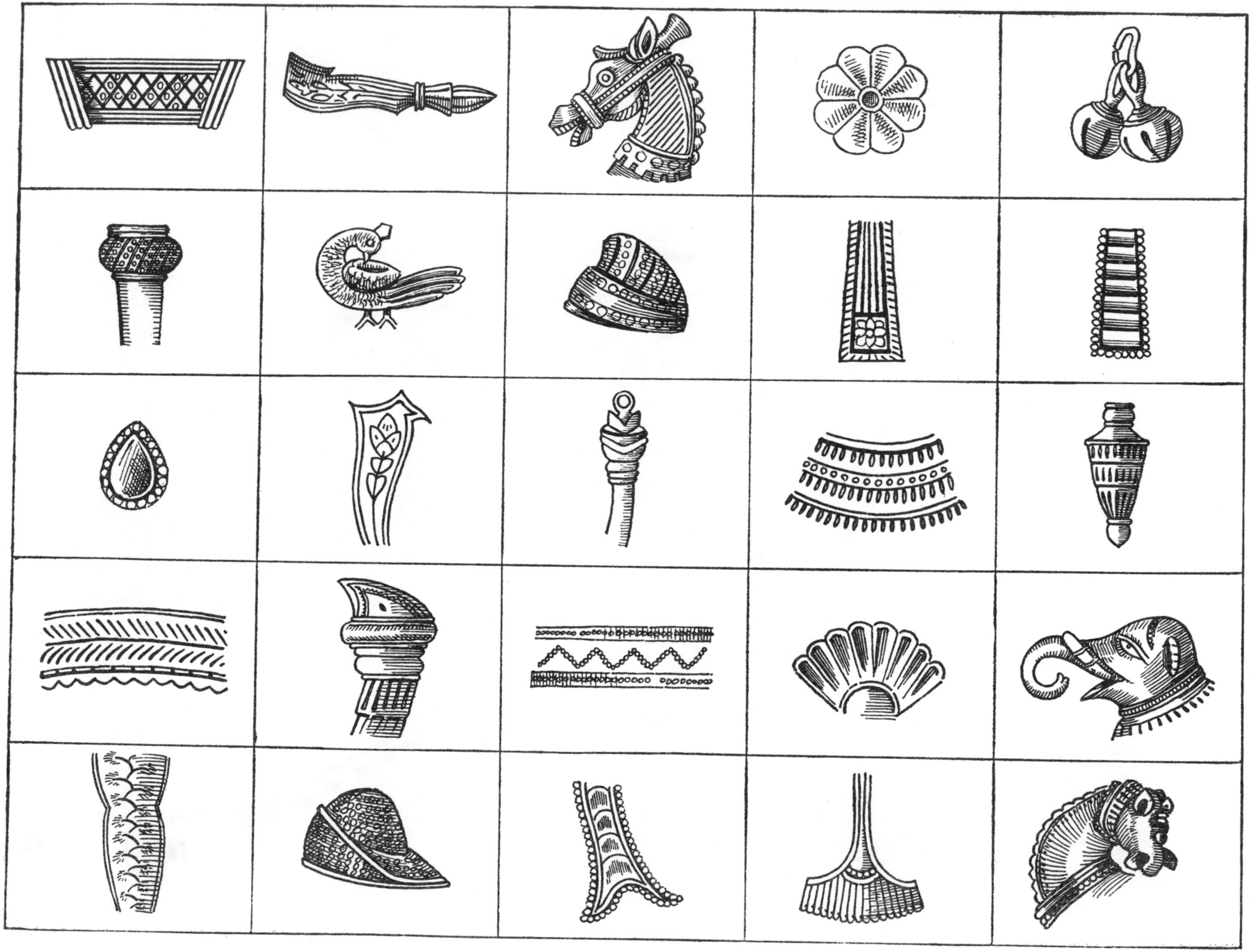

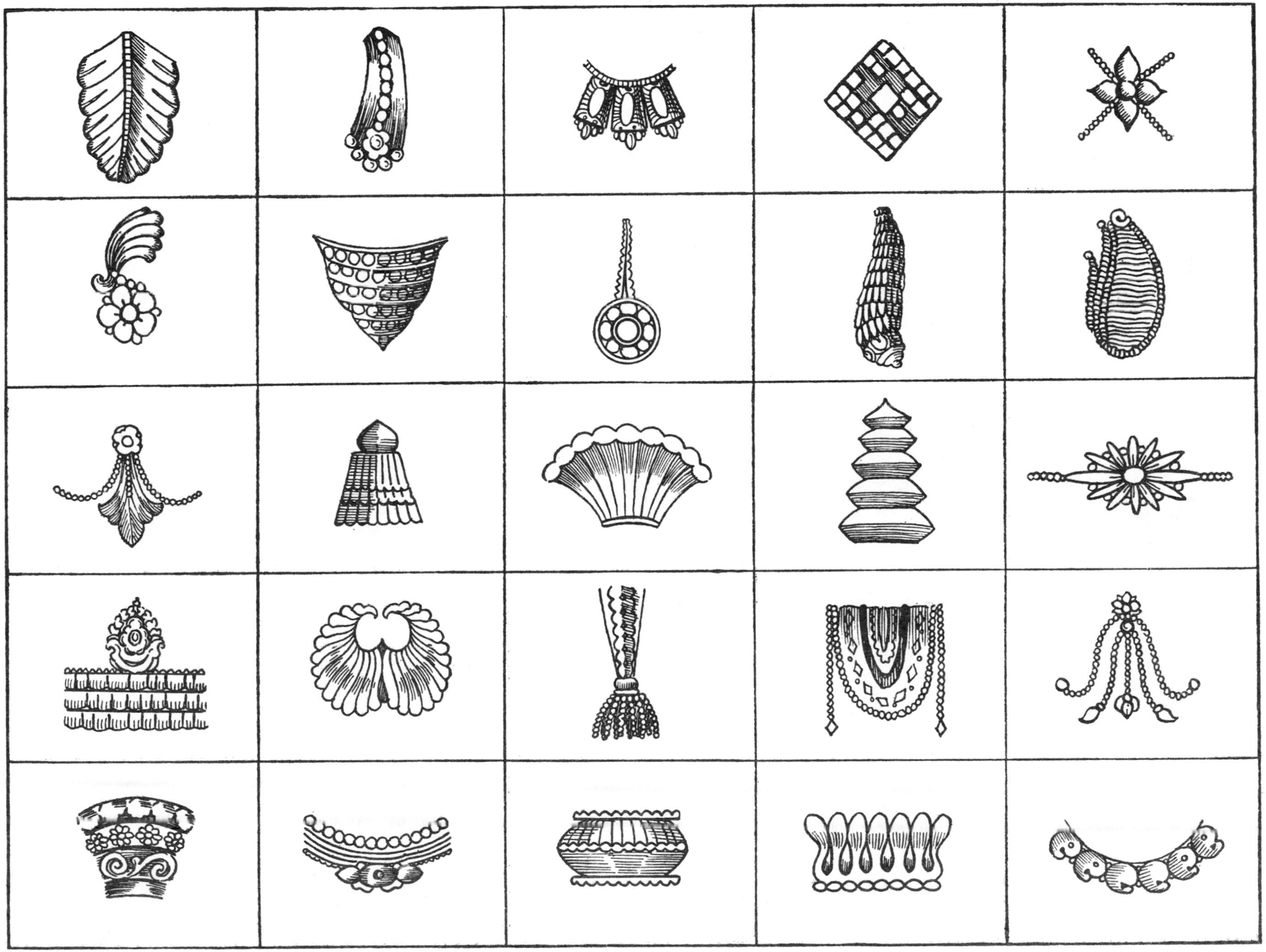

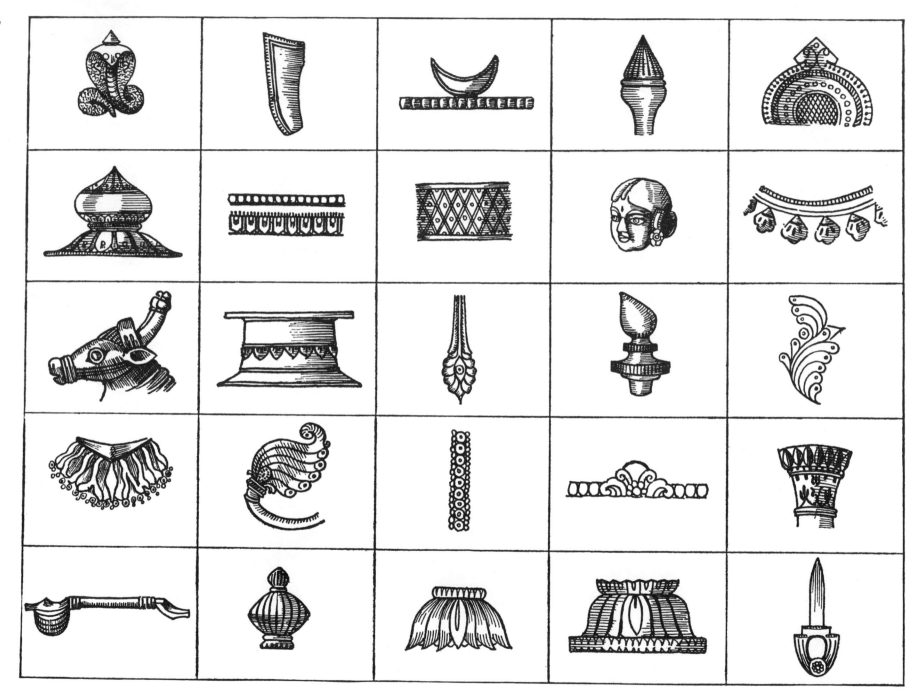

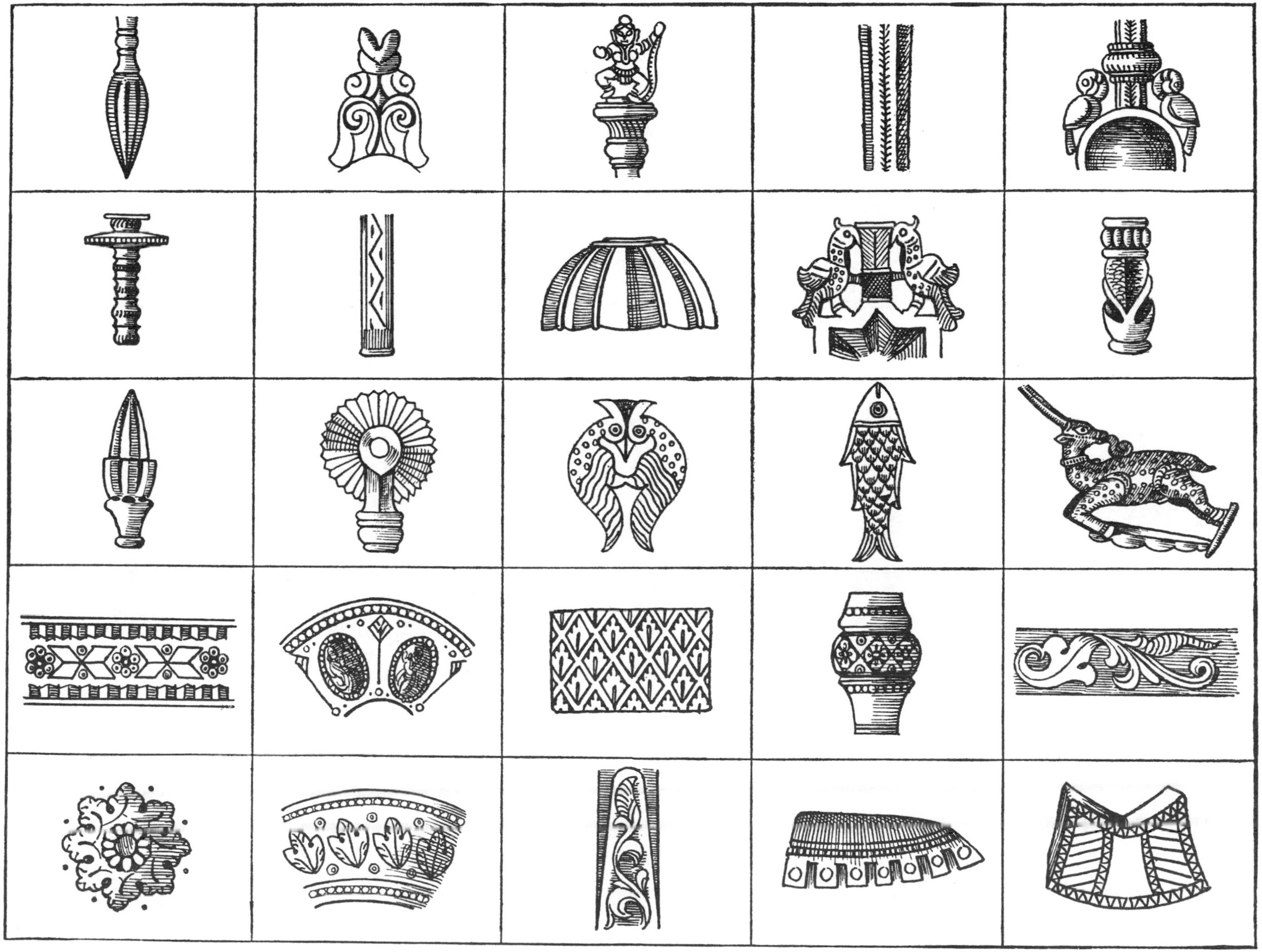

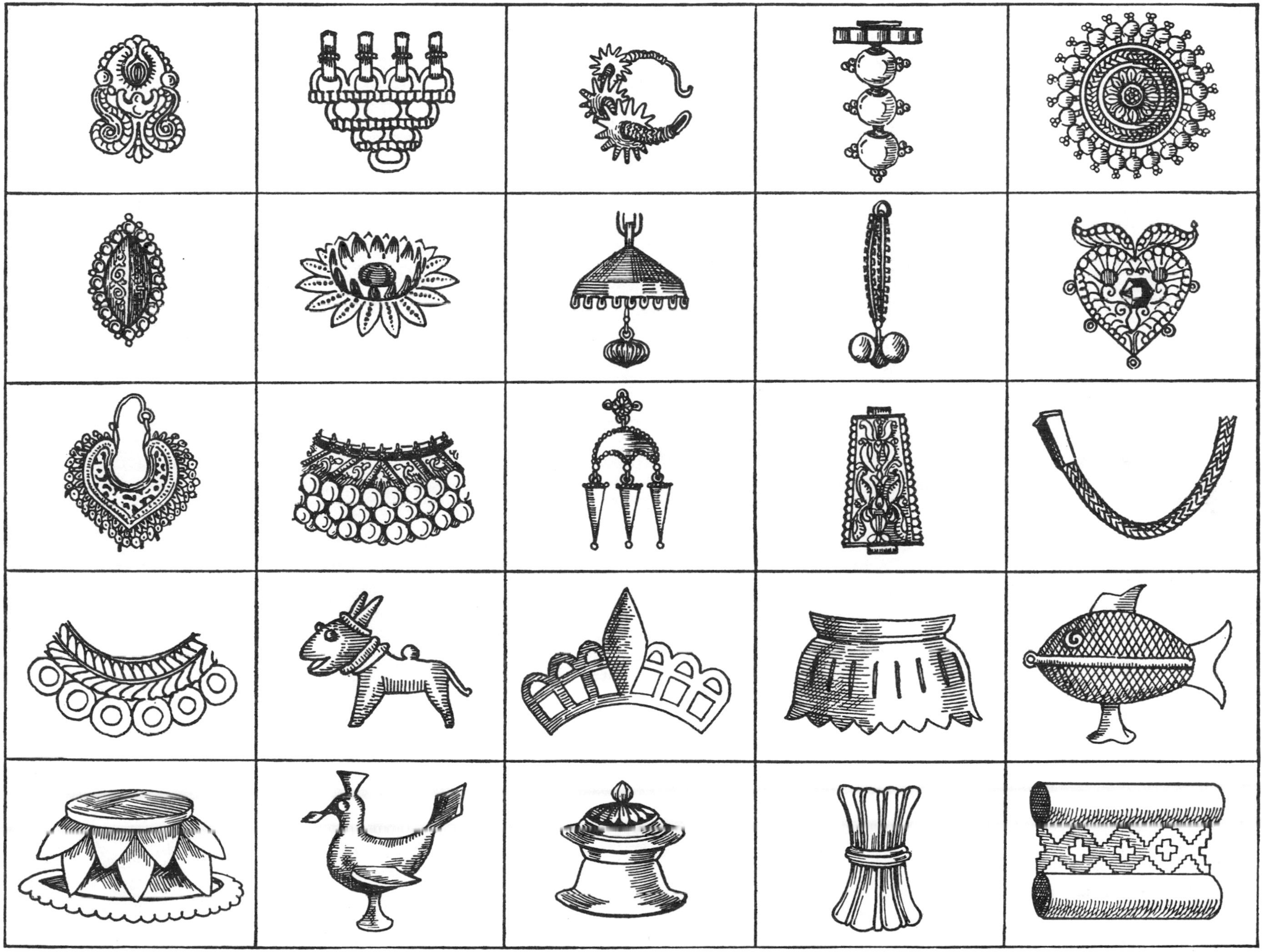

80

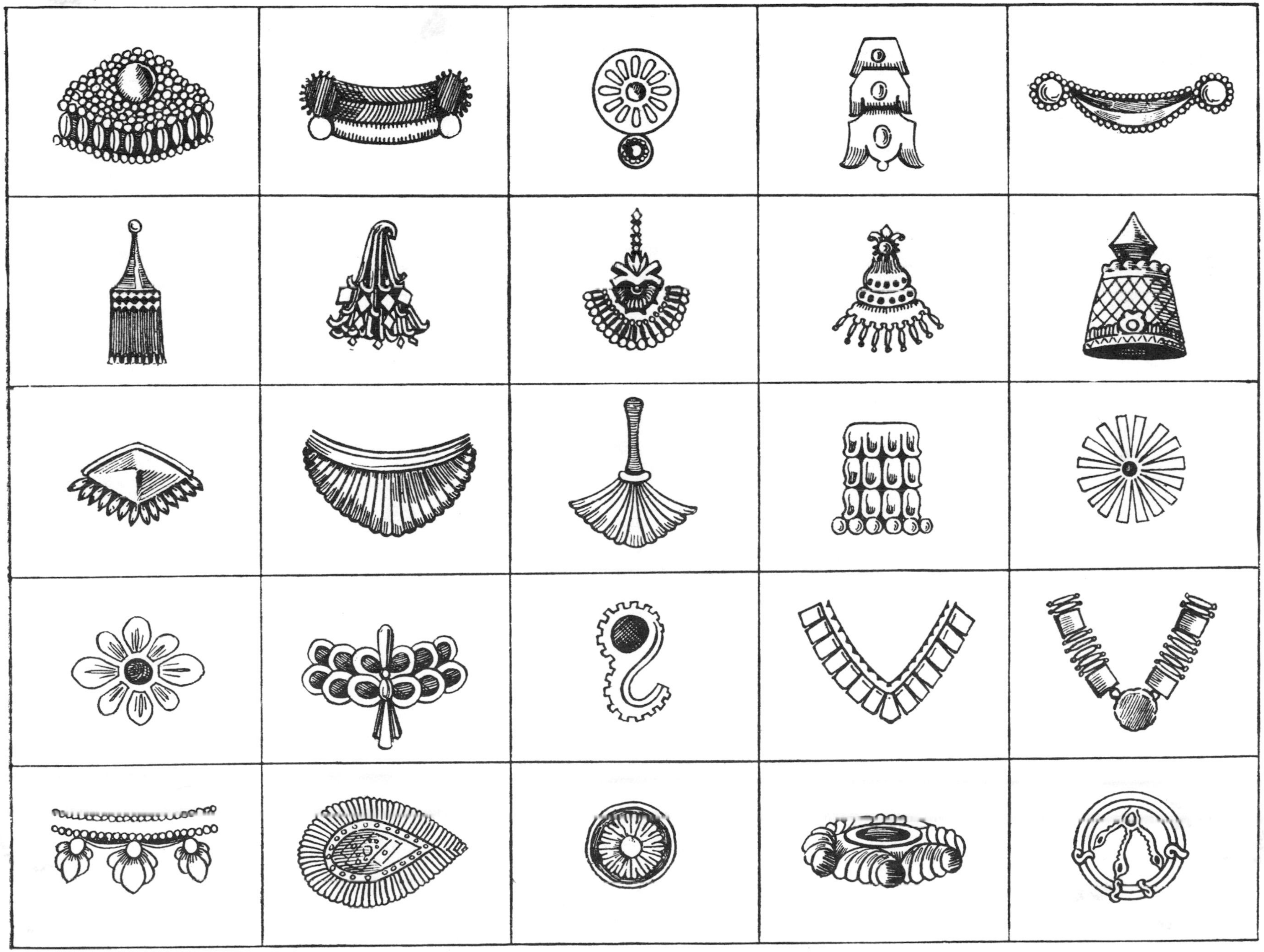

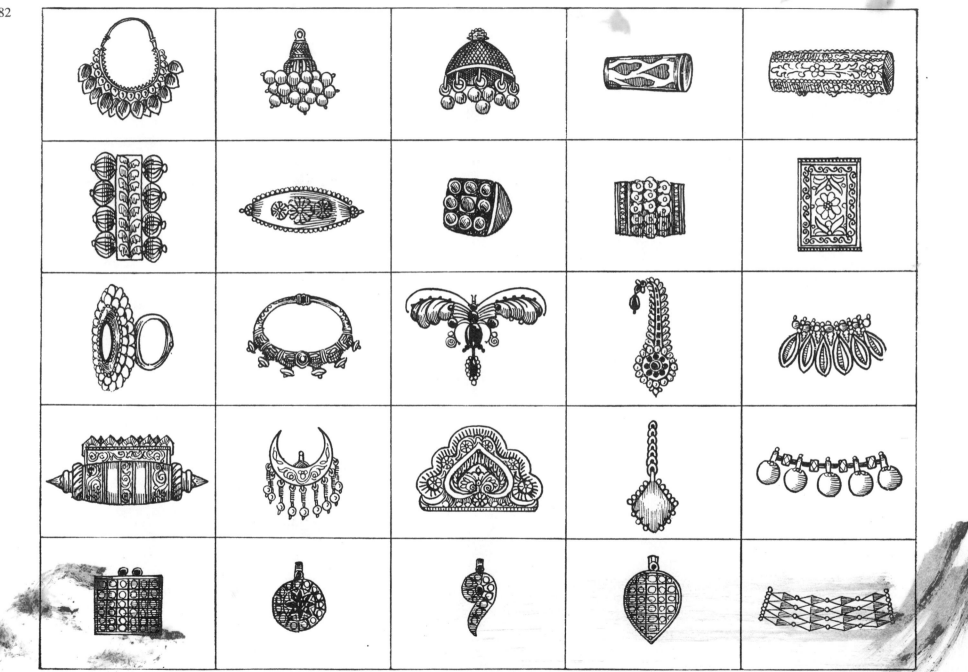

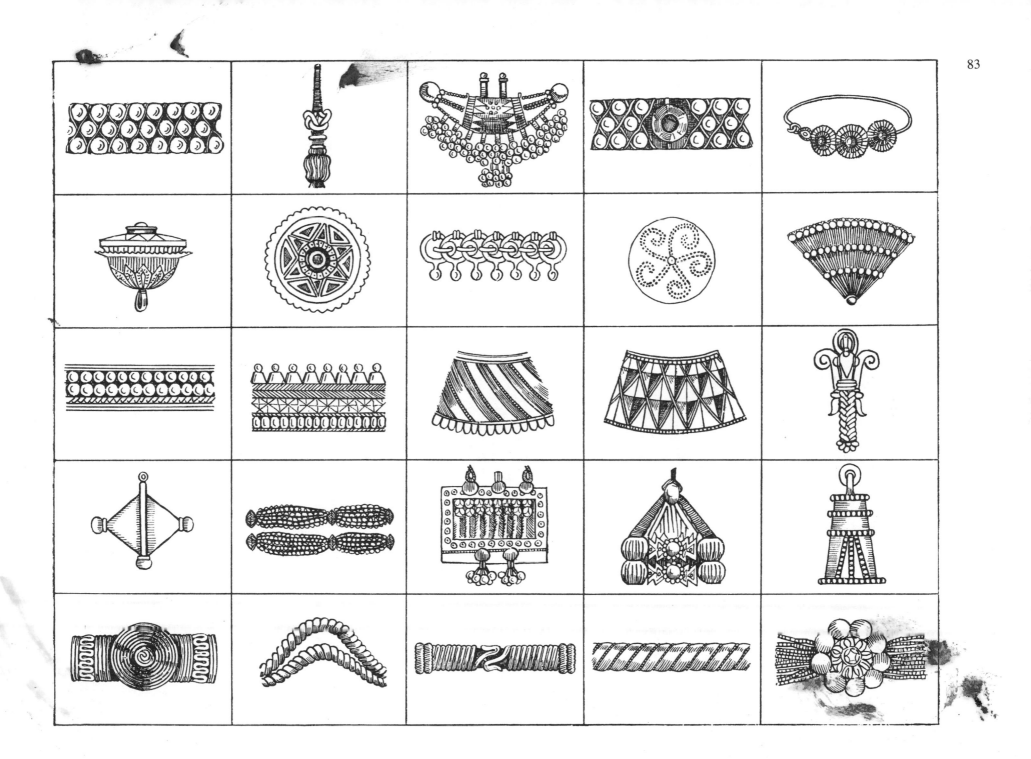

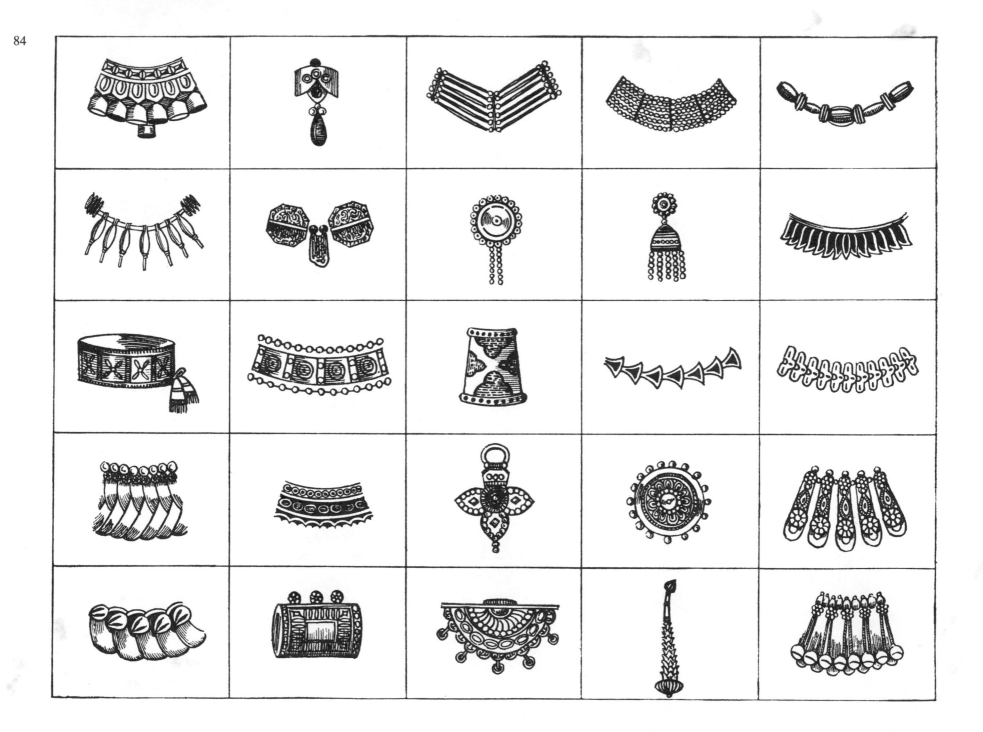

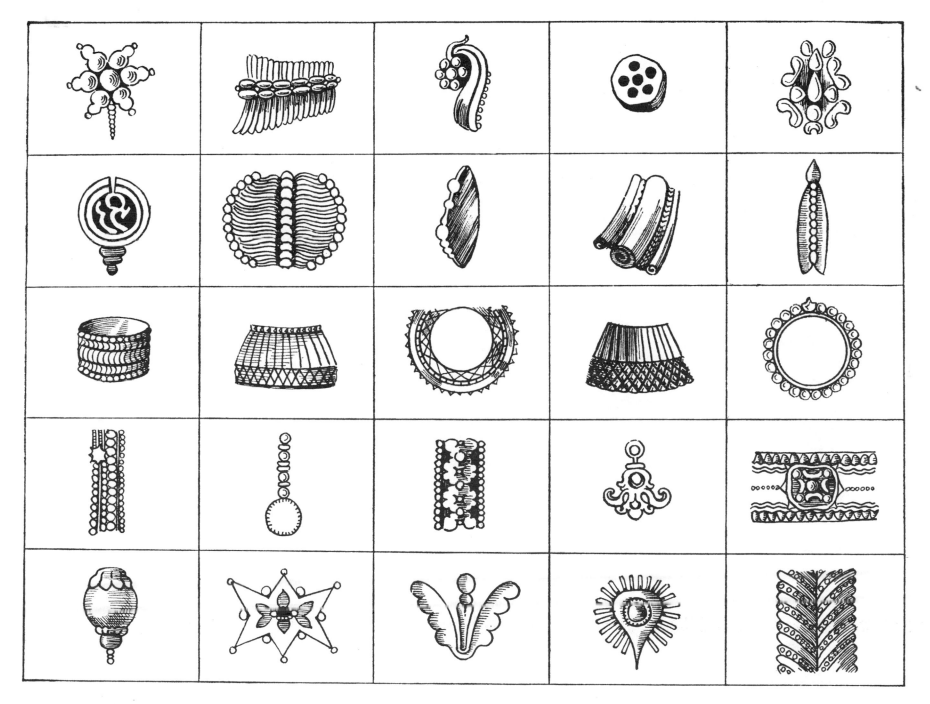

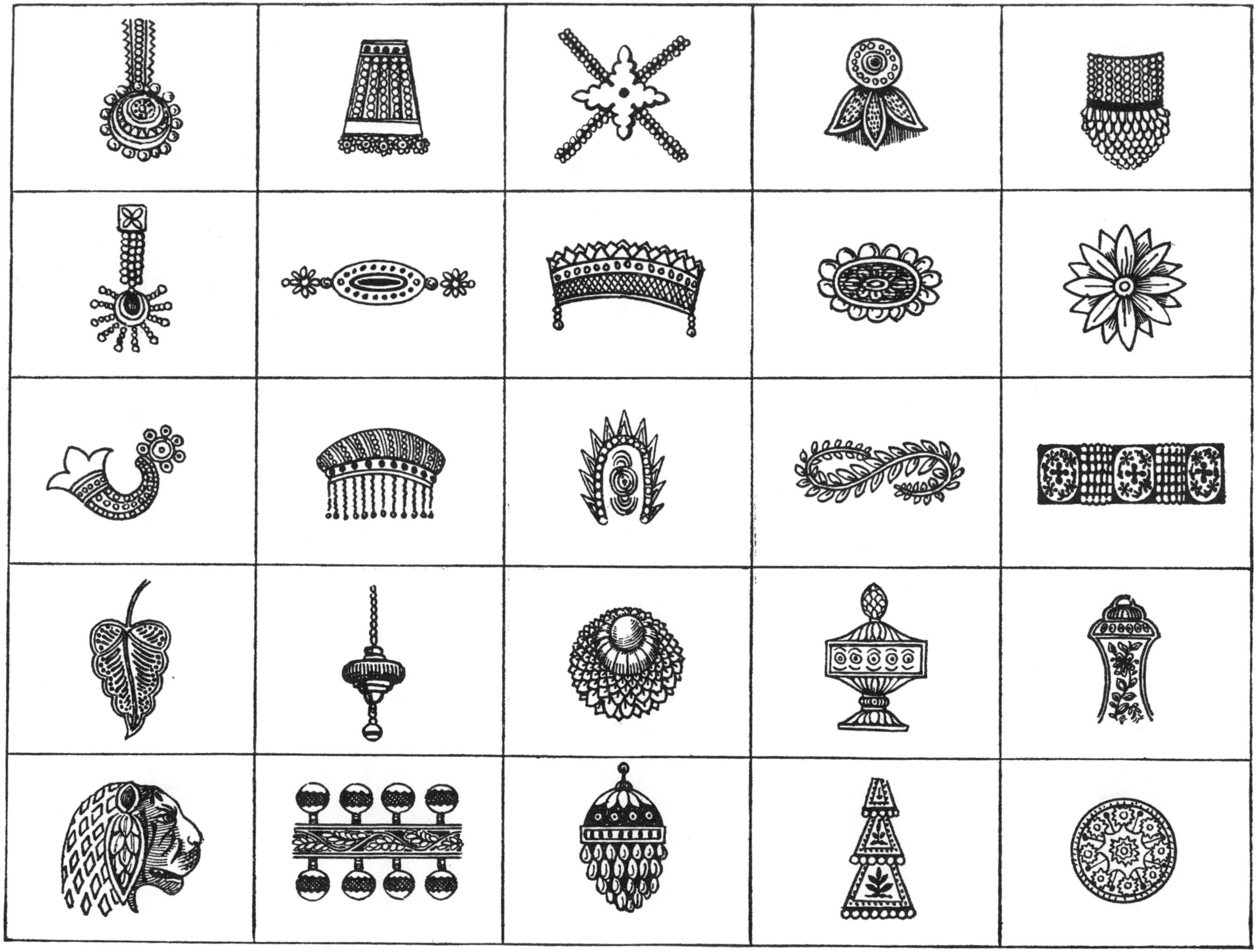

87

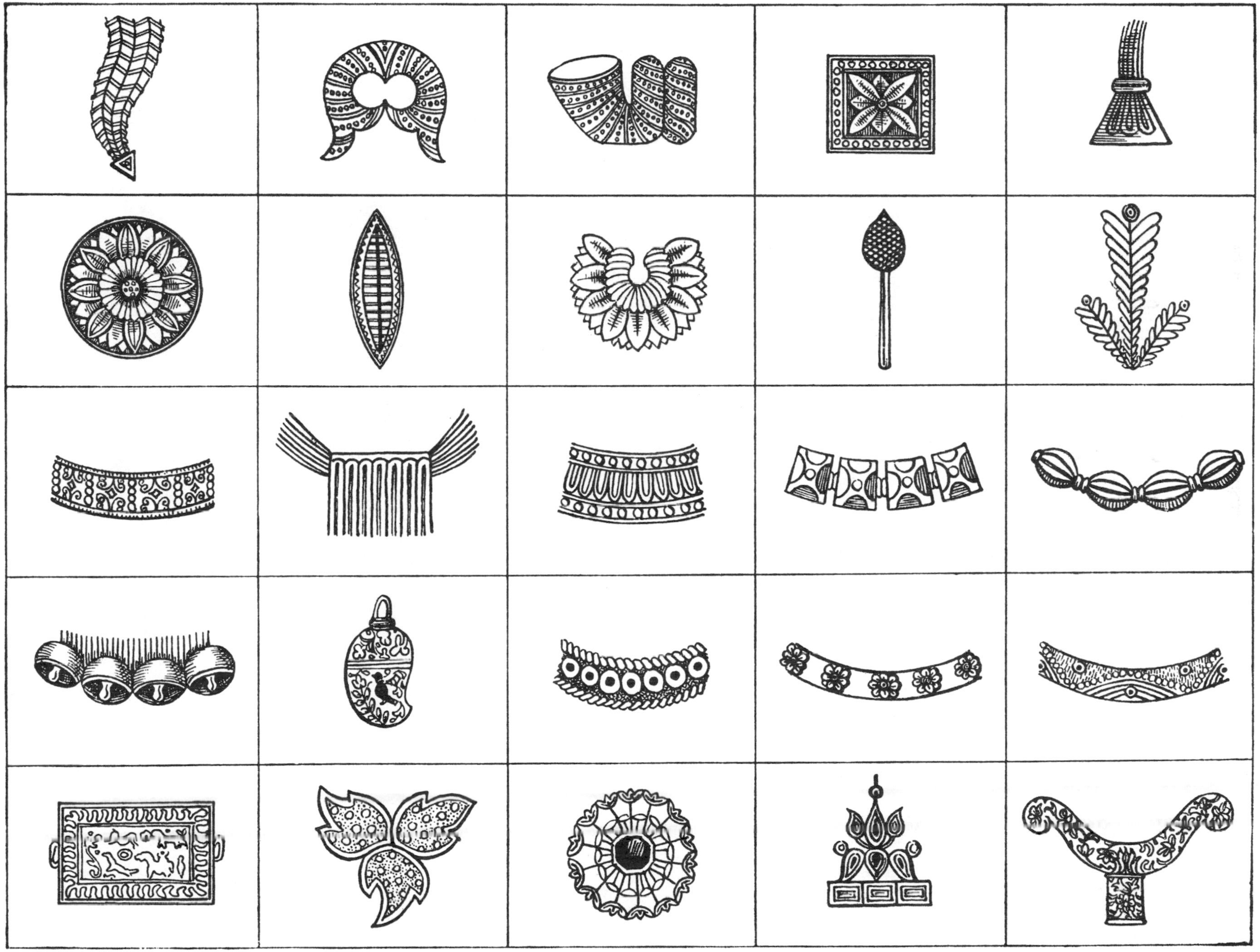

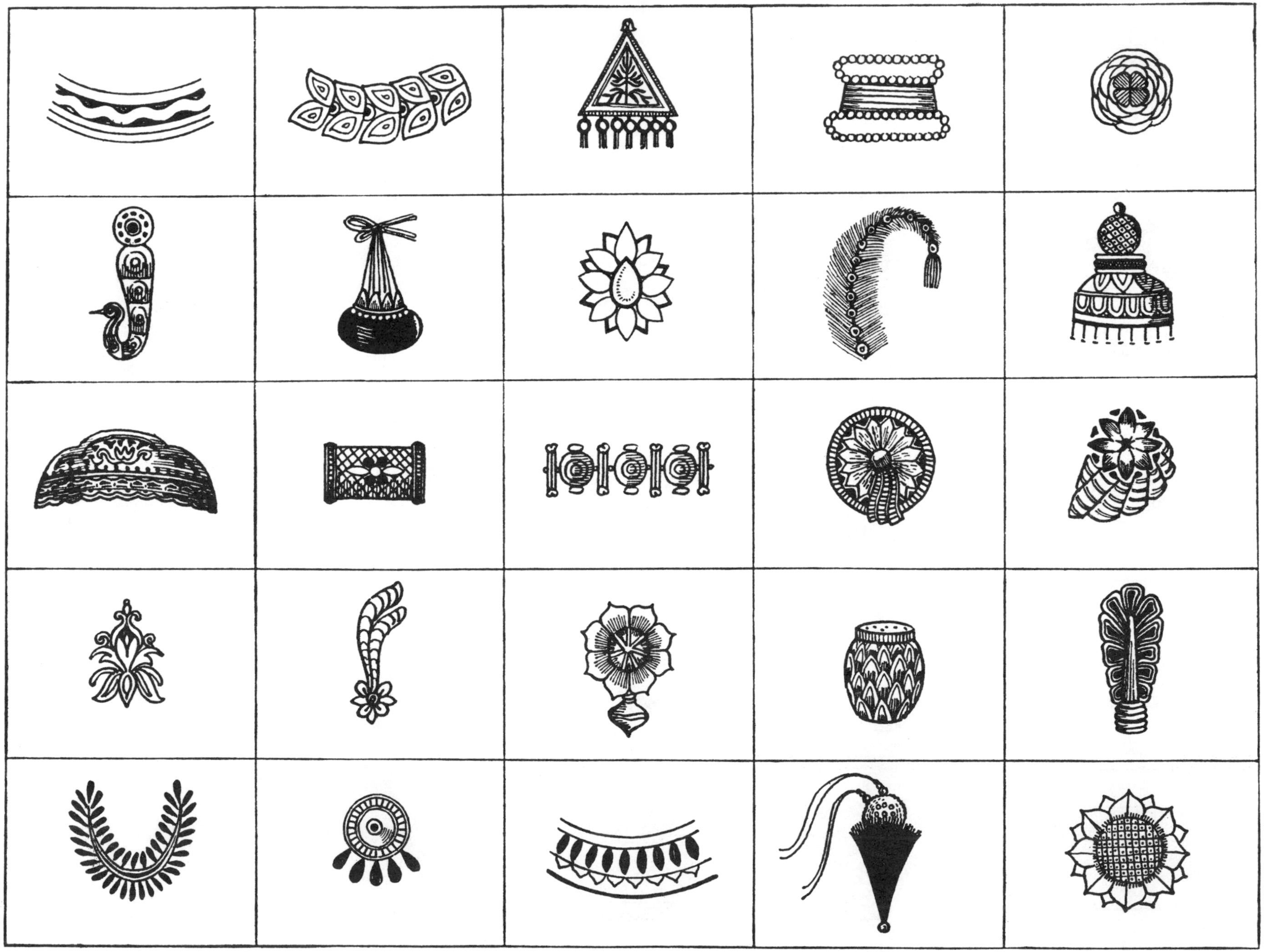

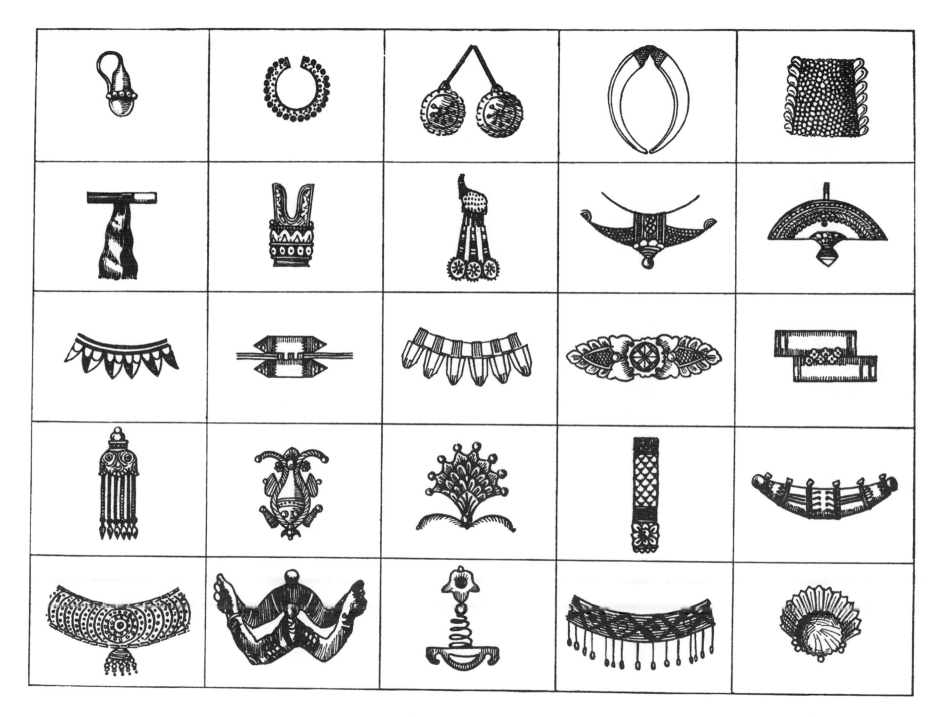

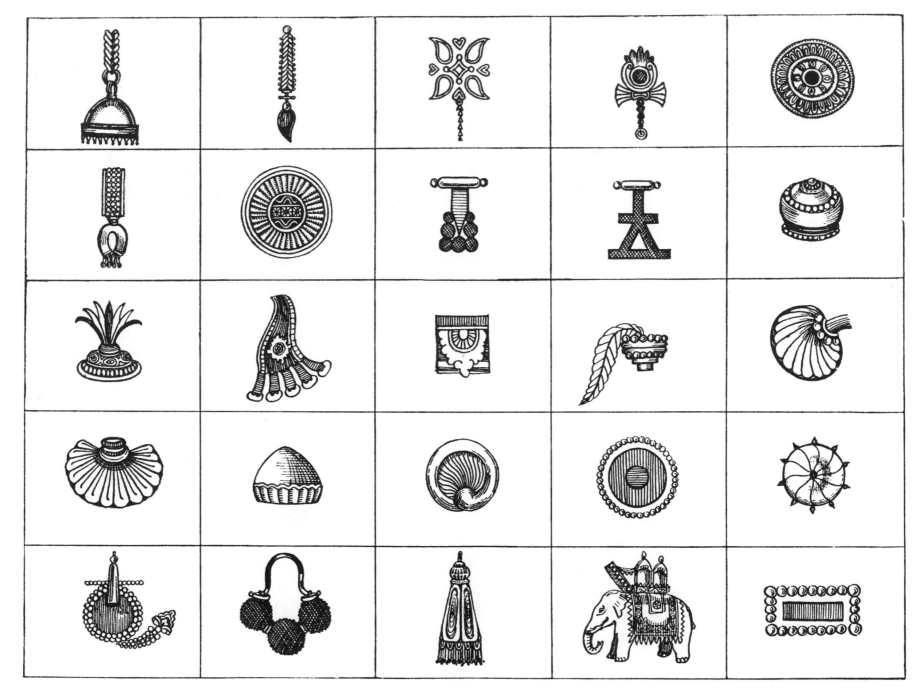

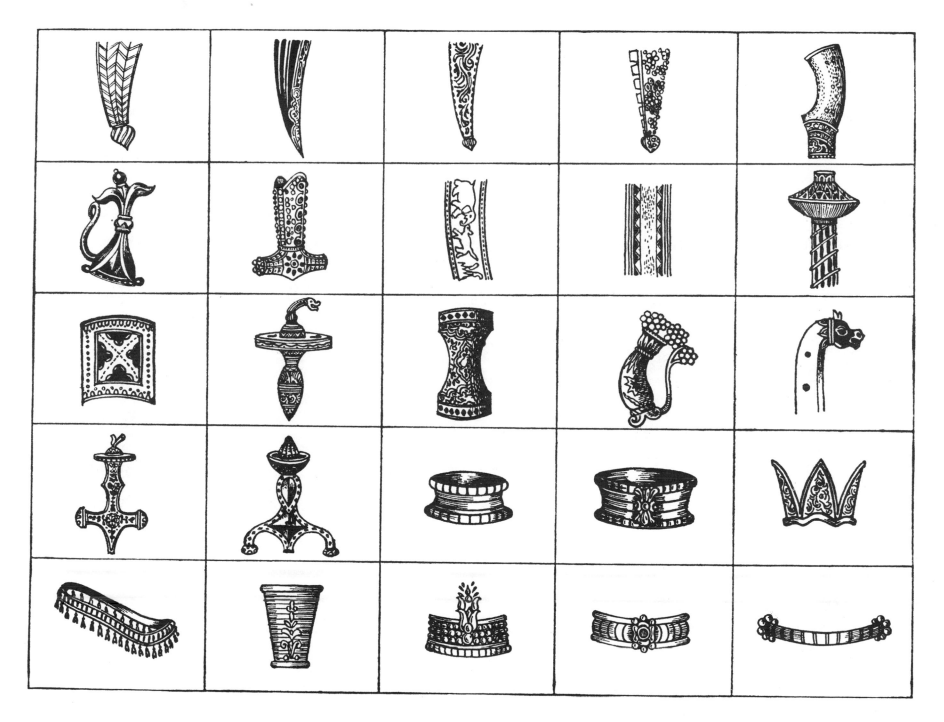

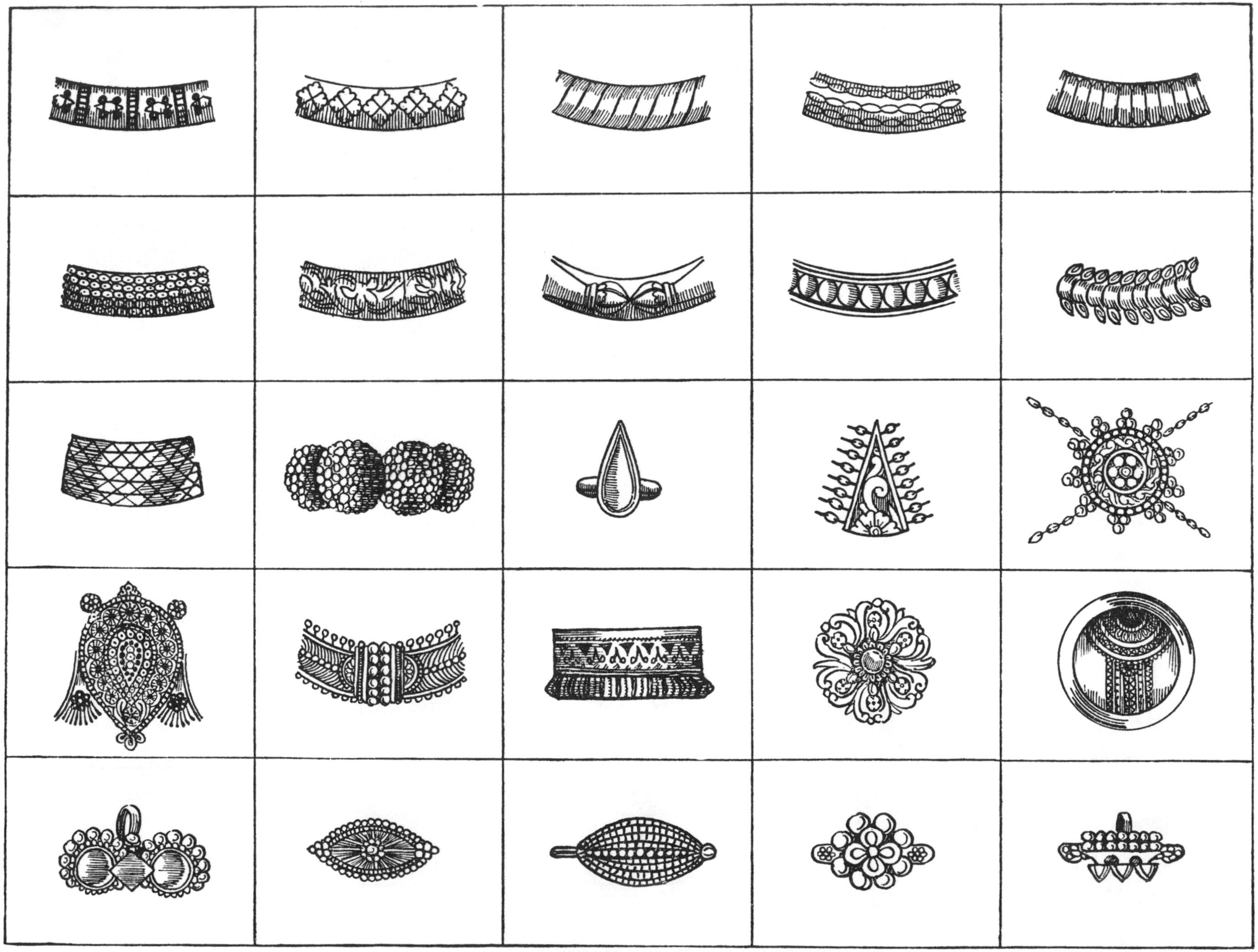

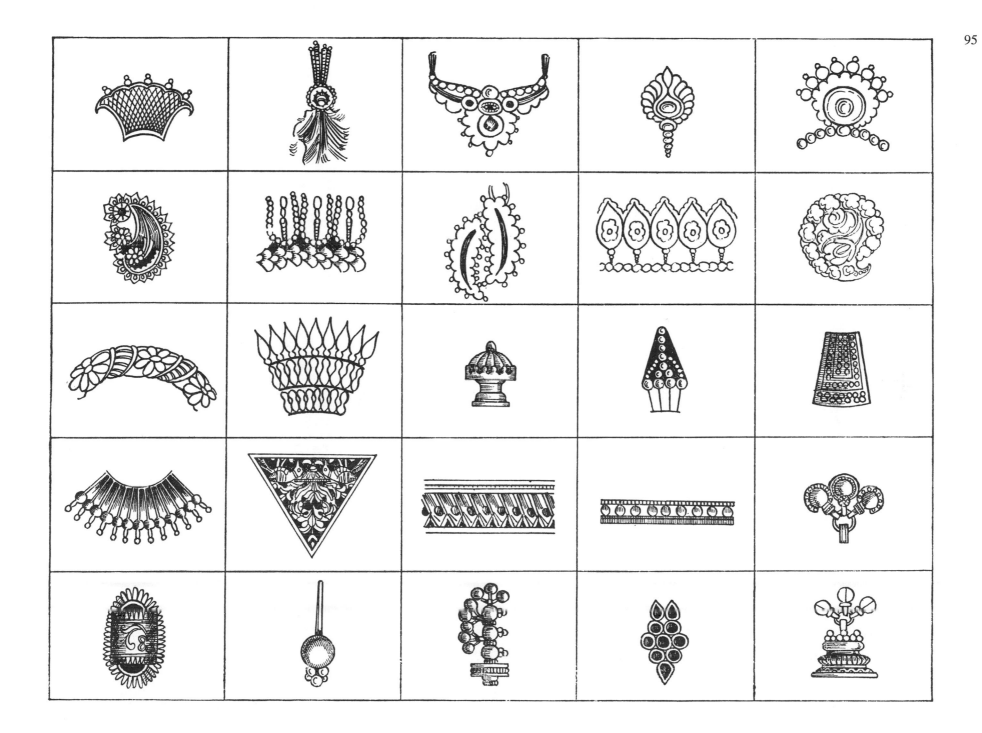

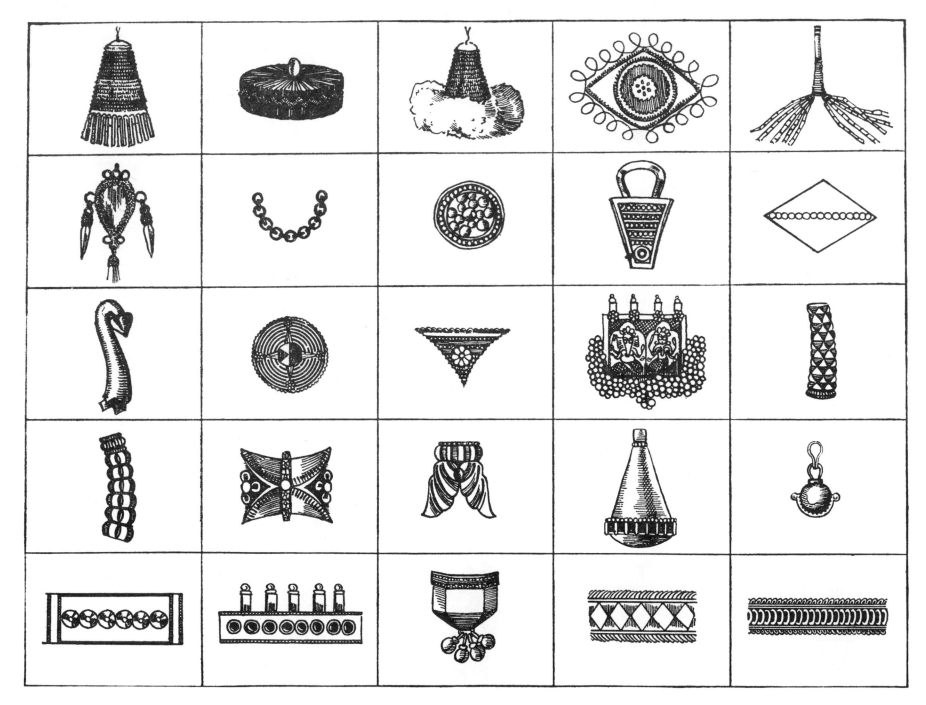

96

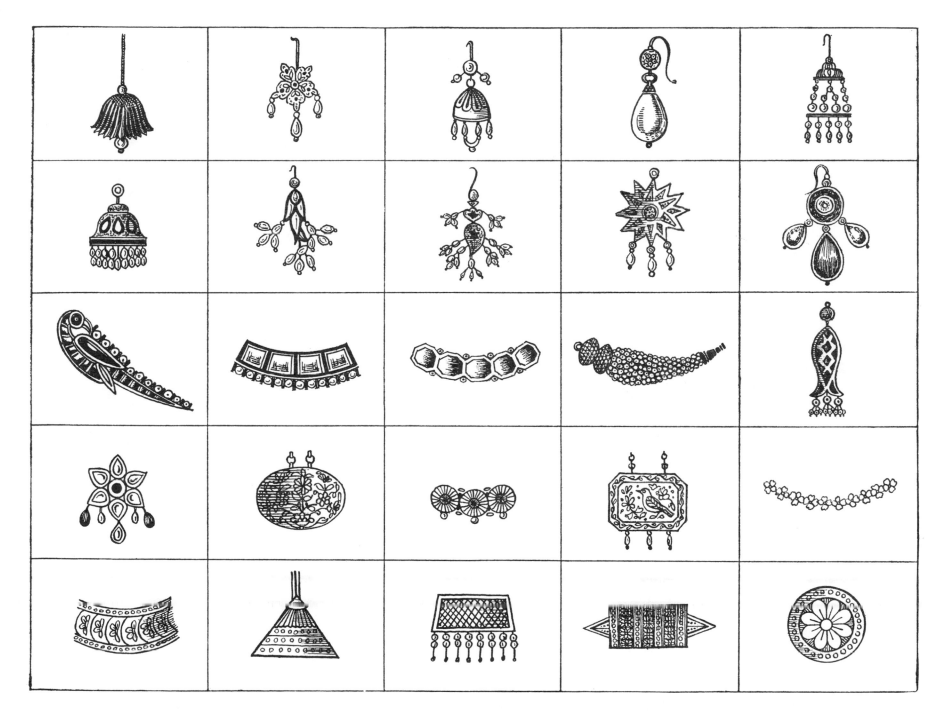

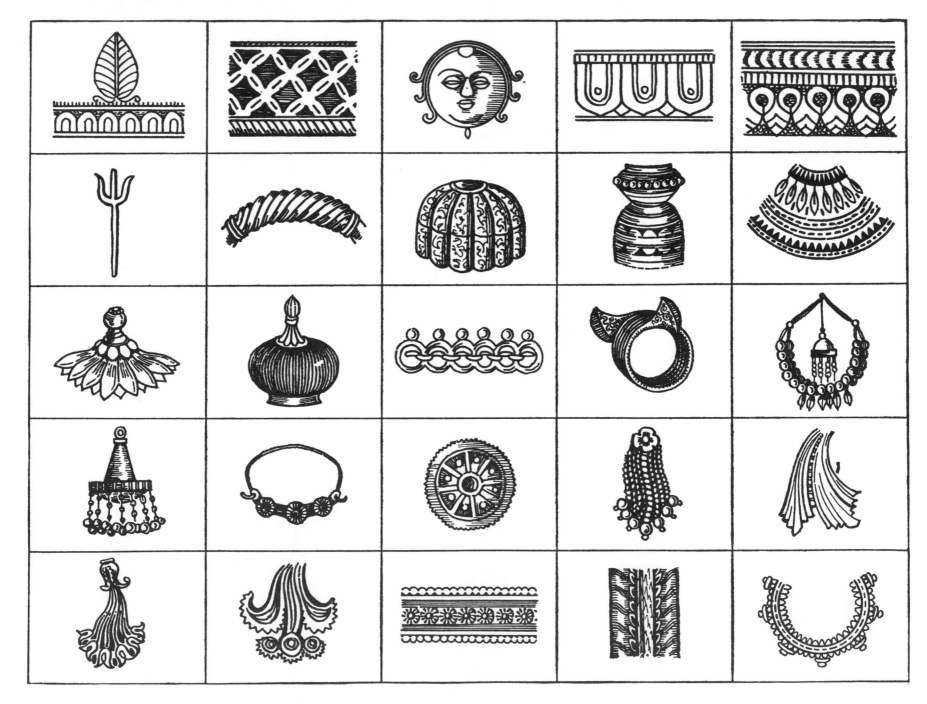

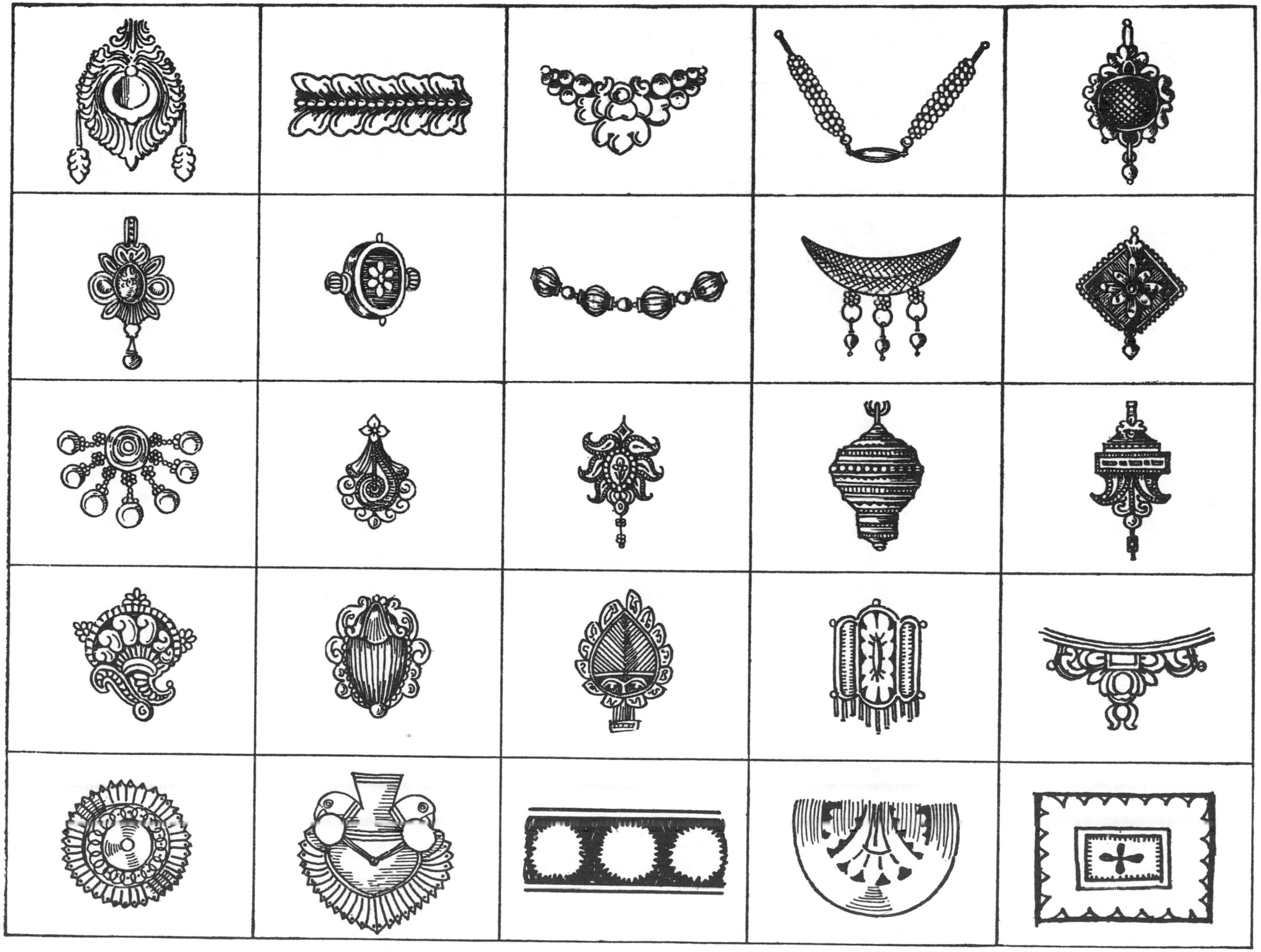

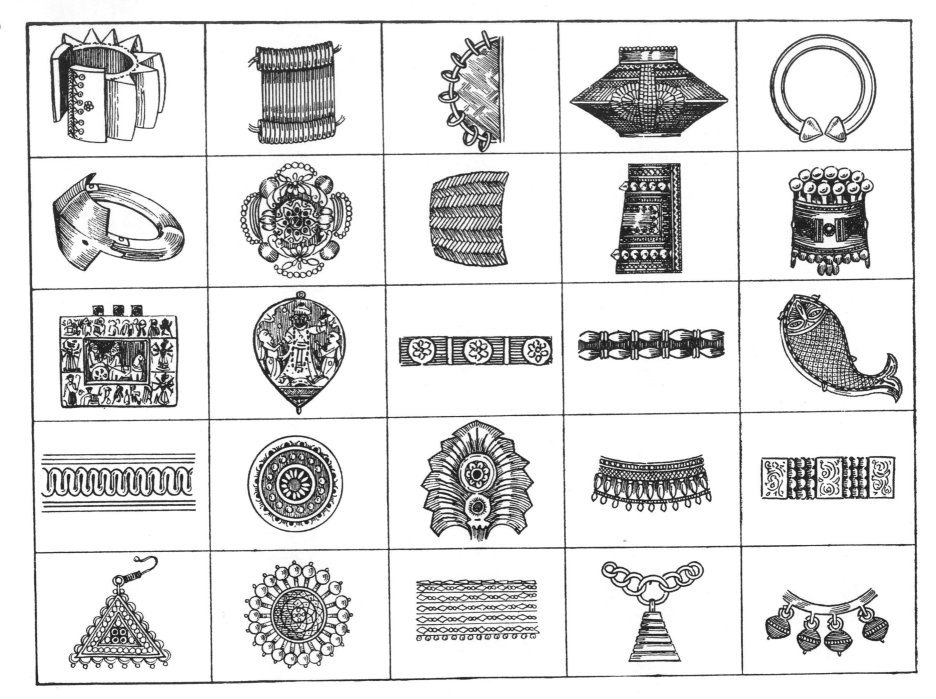

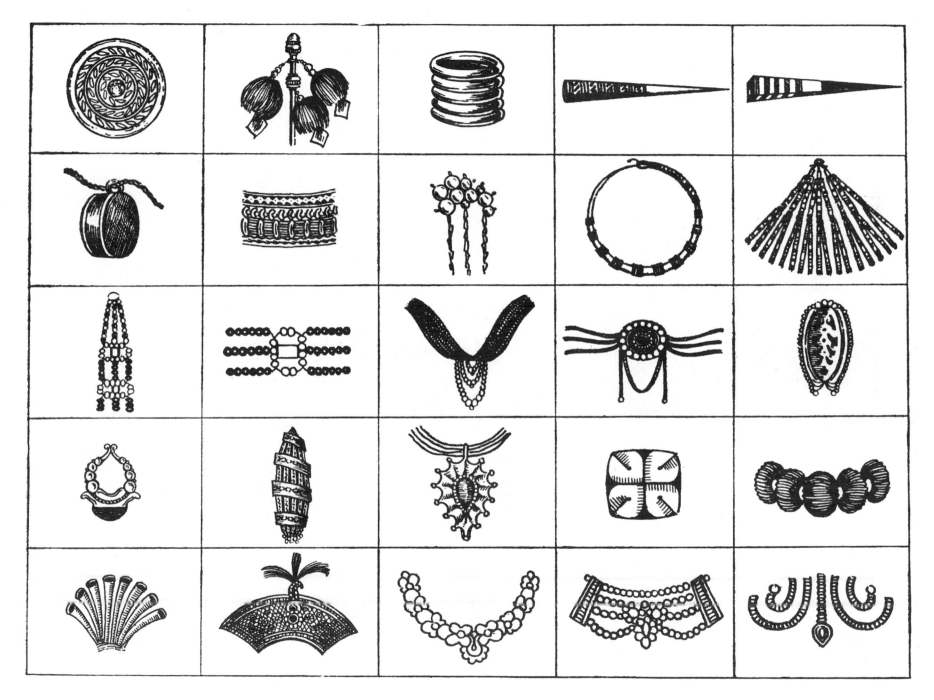

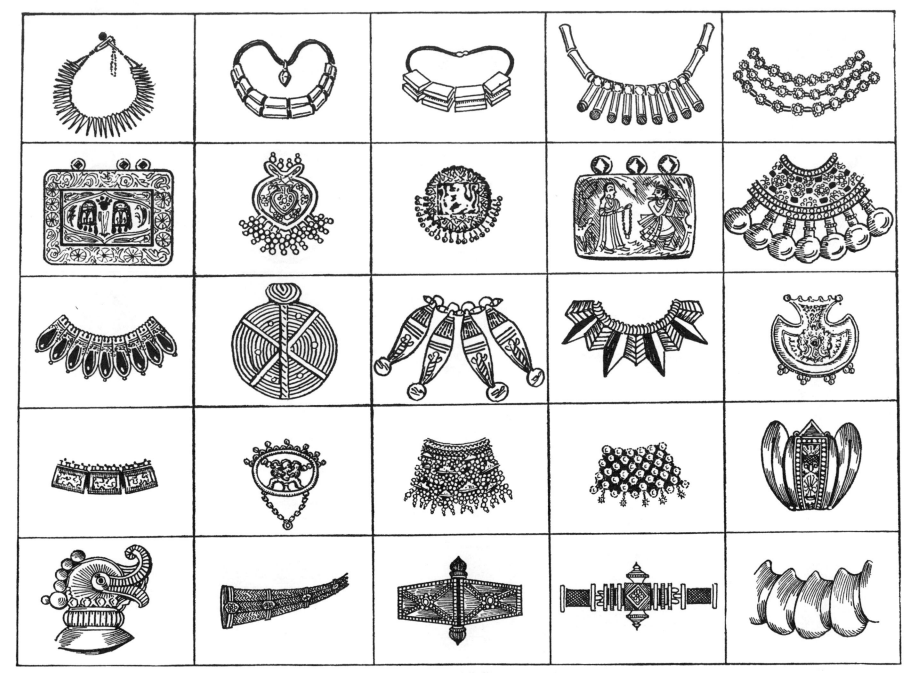

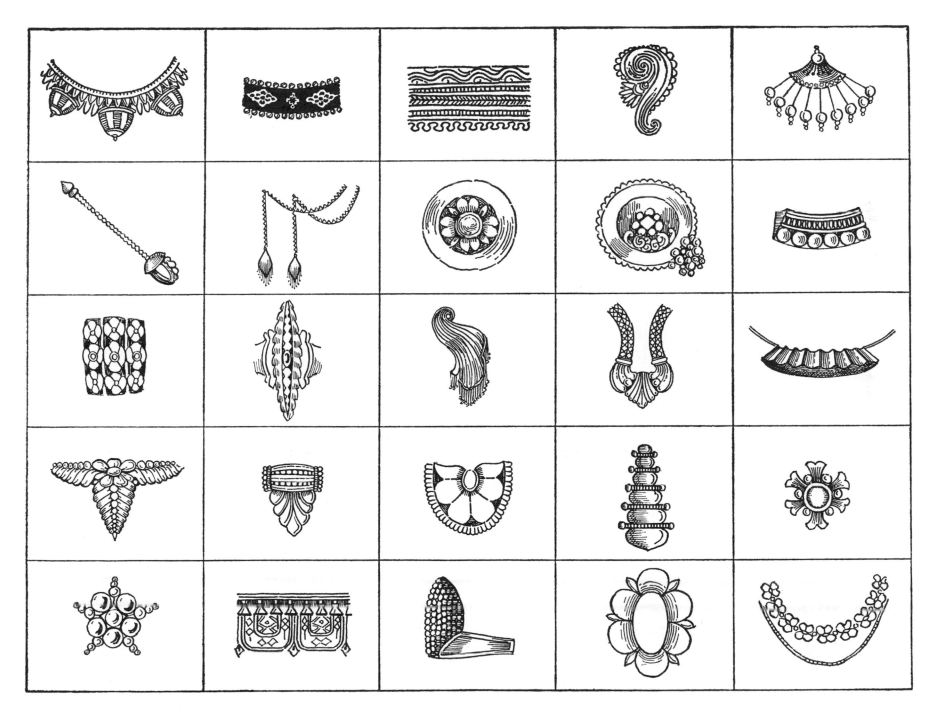

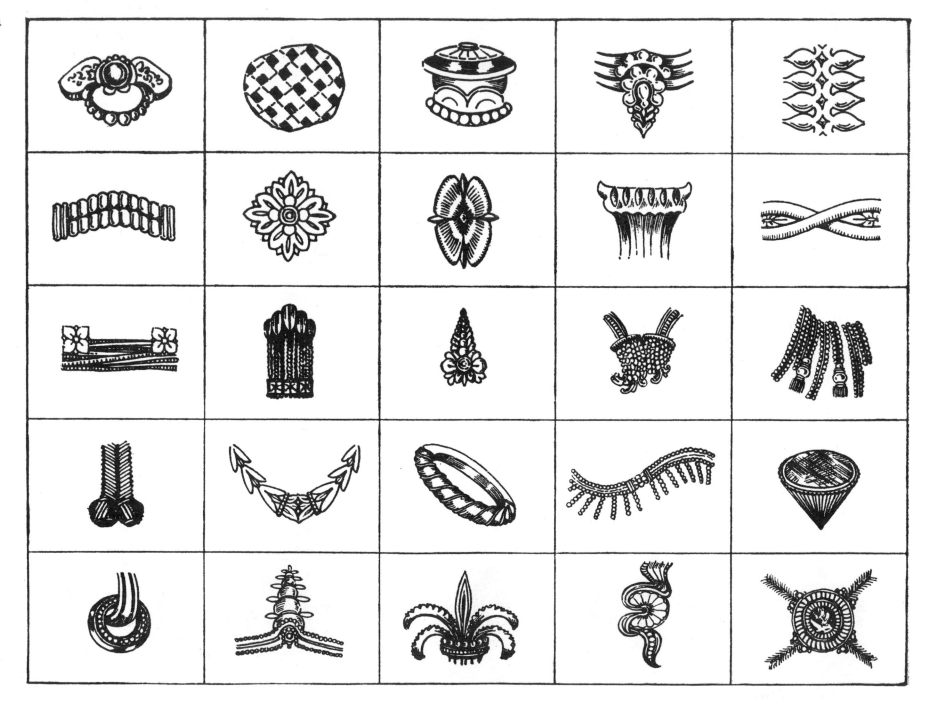

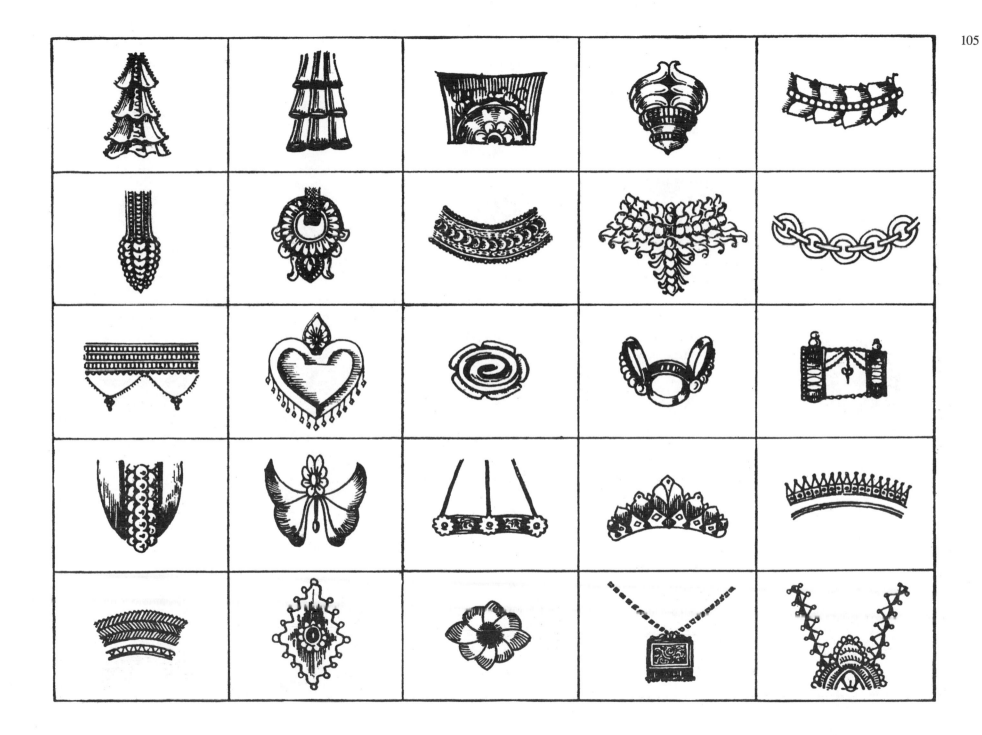

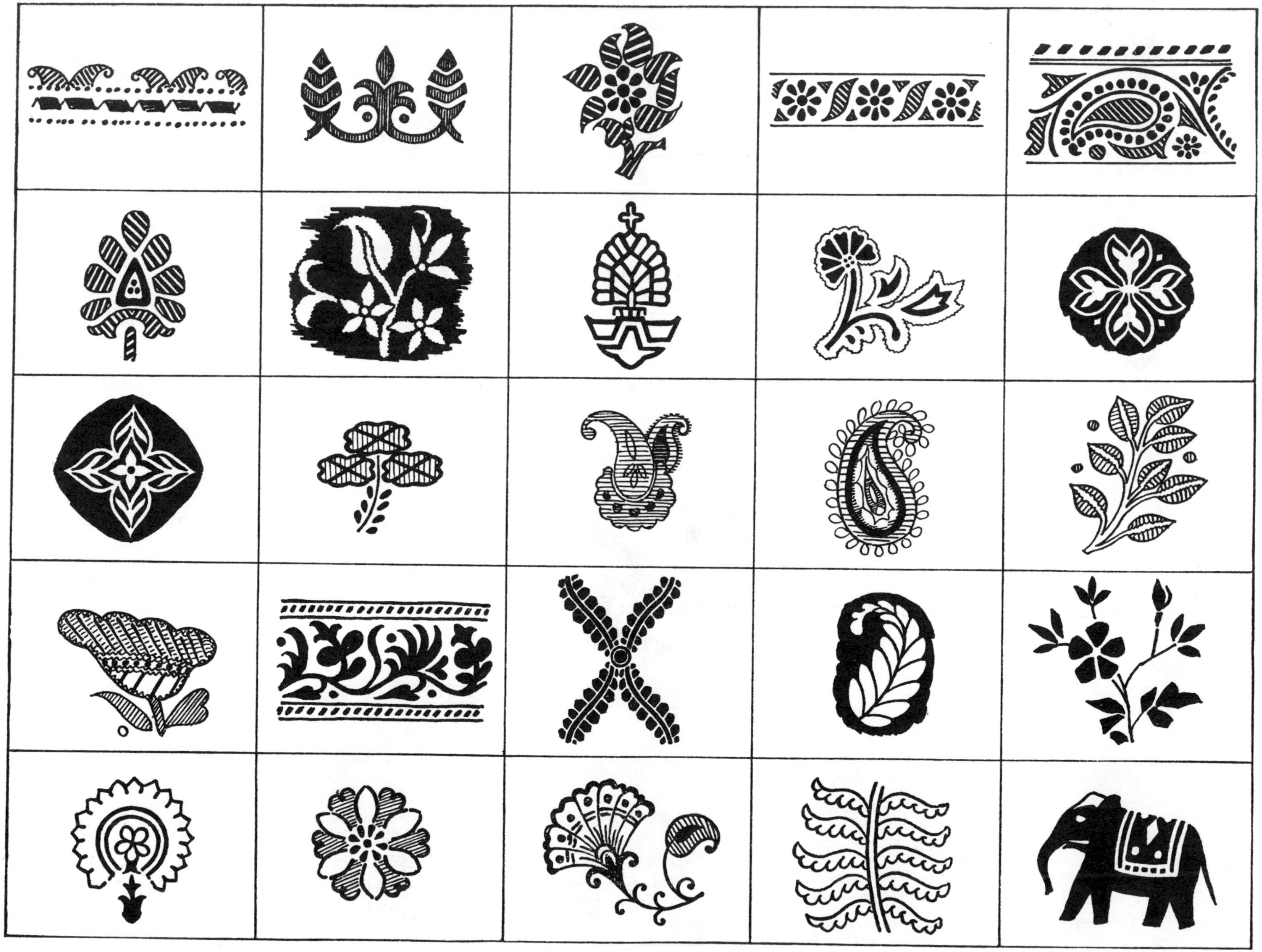

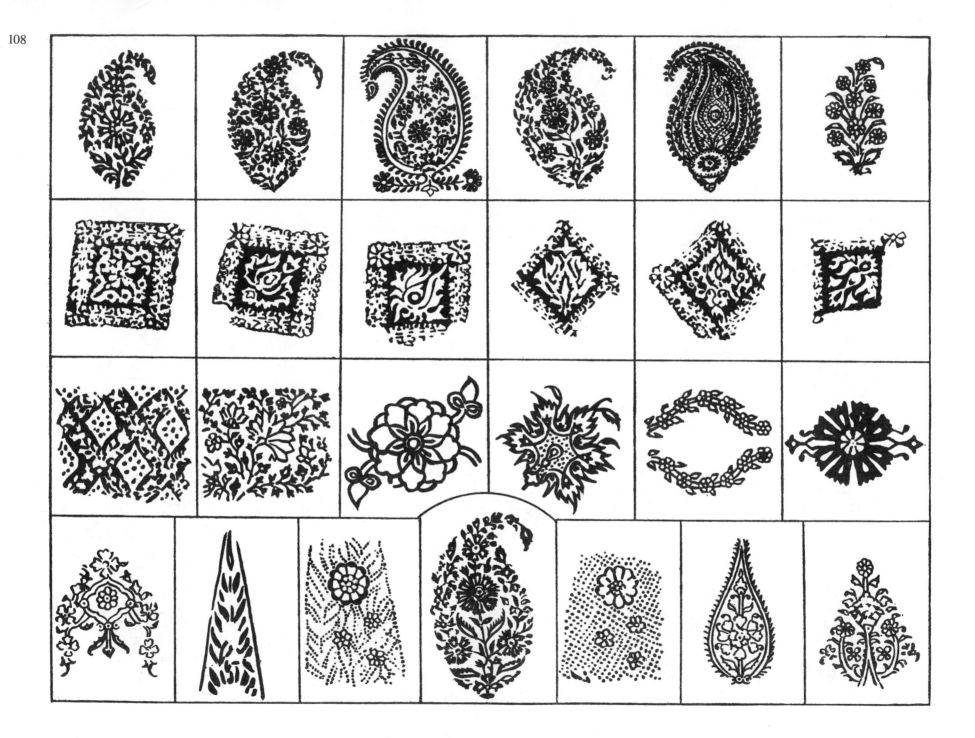

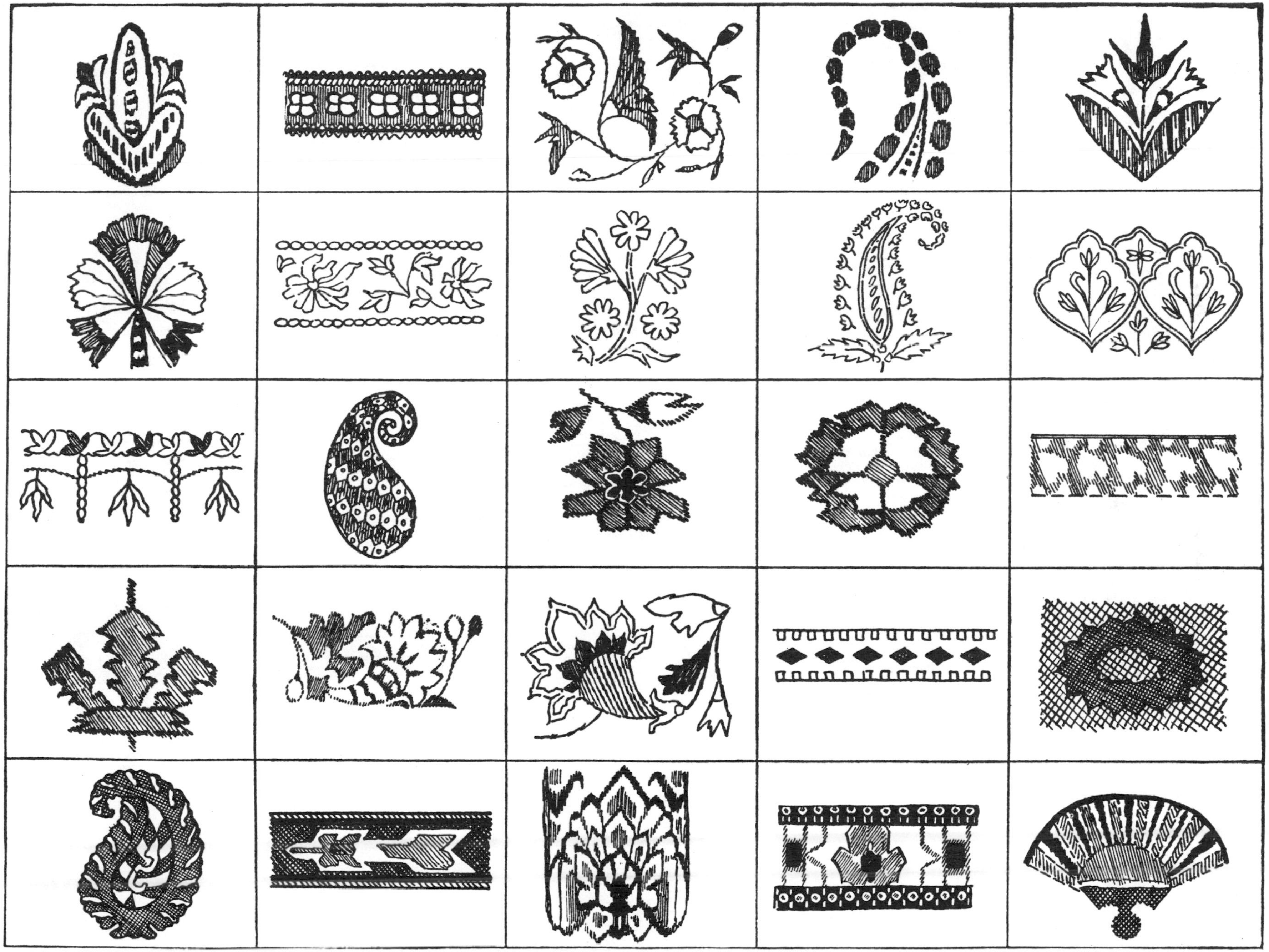

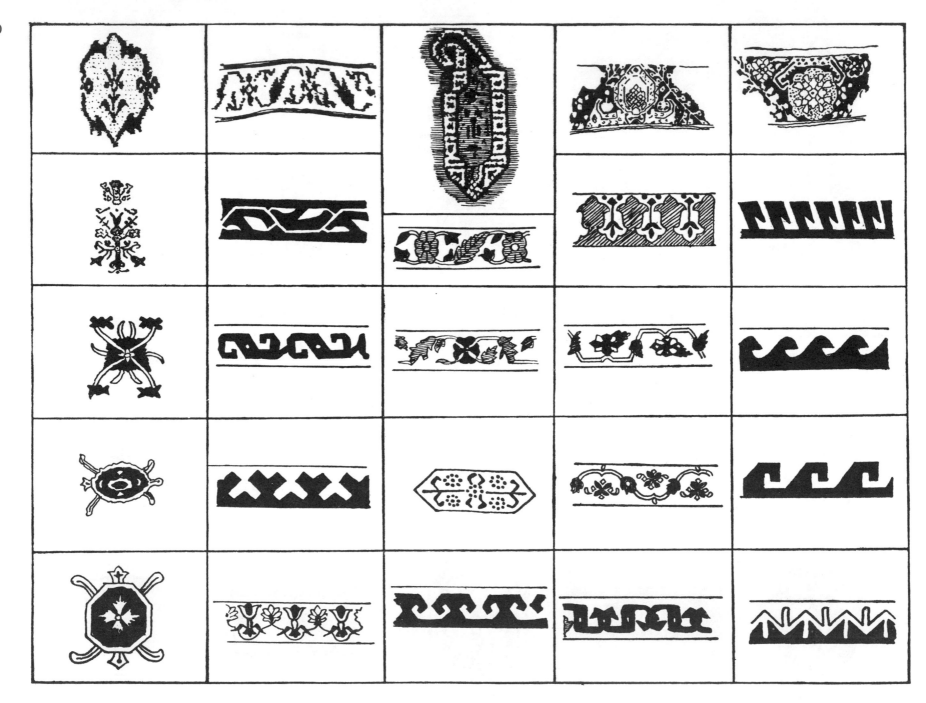

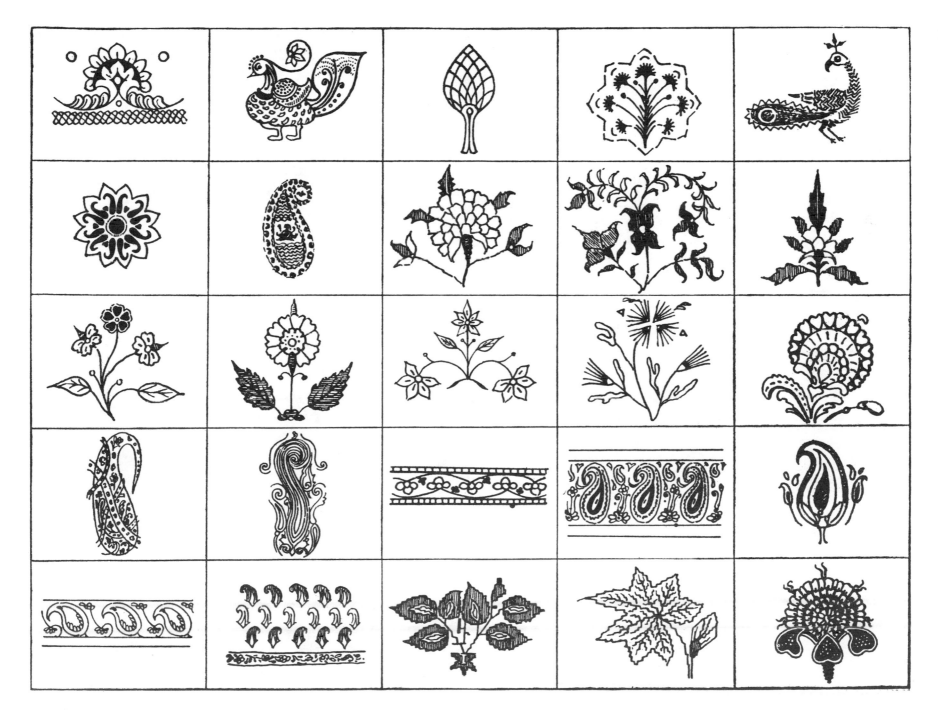

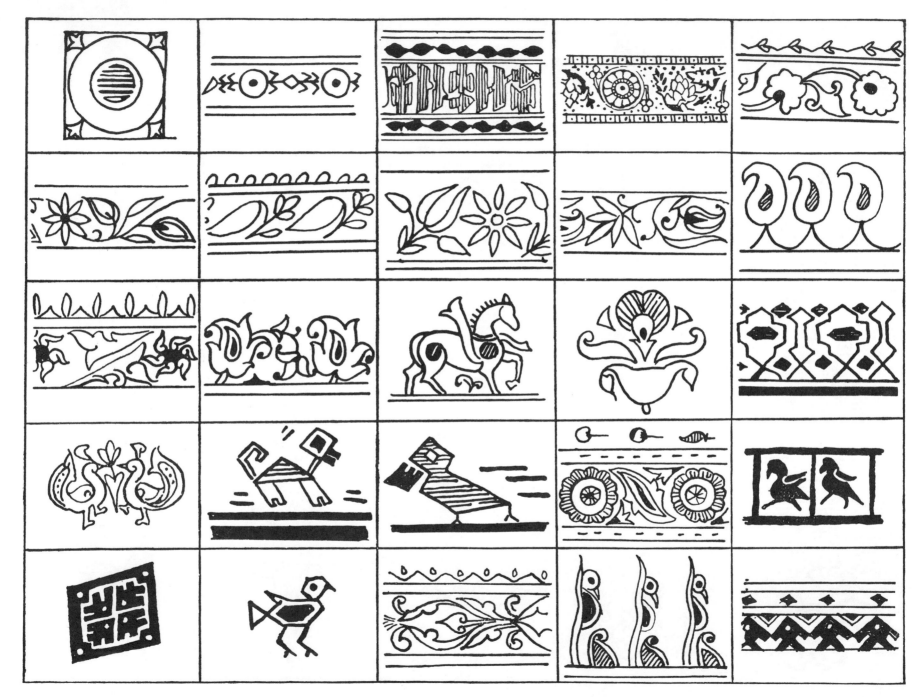

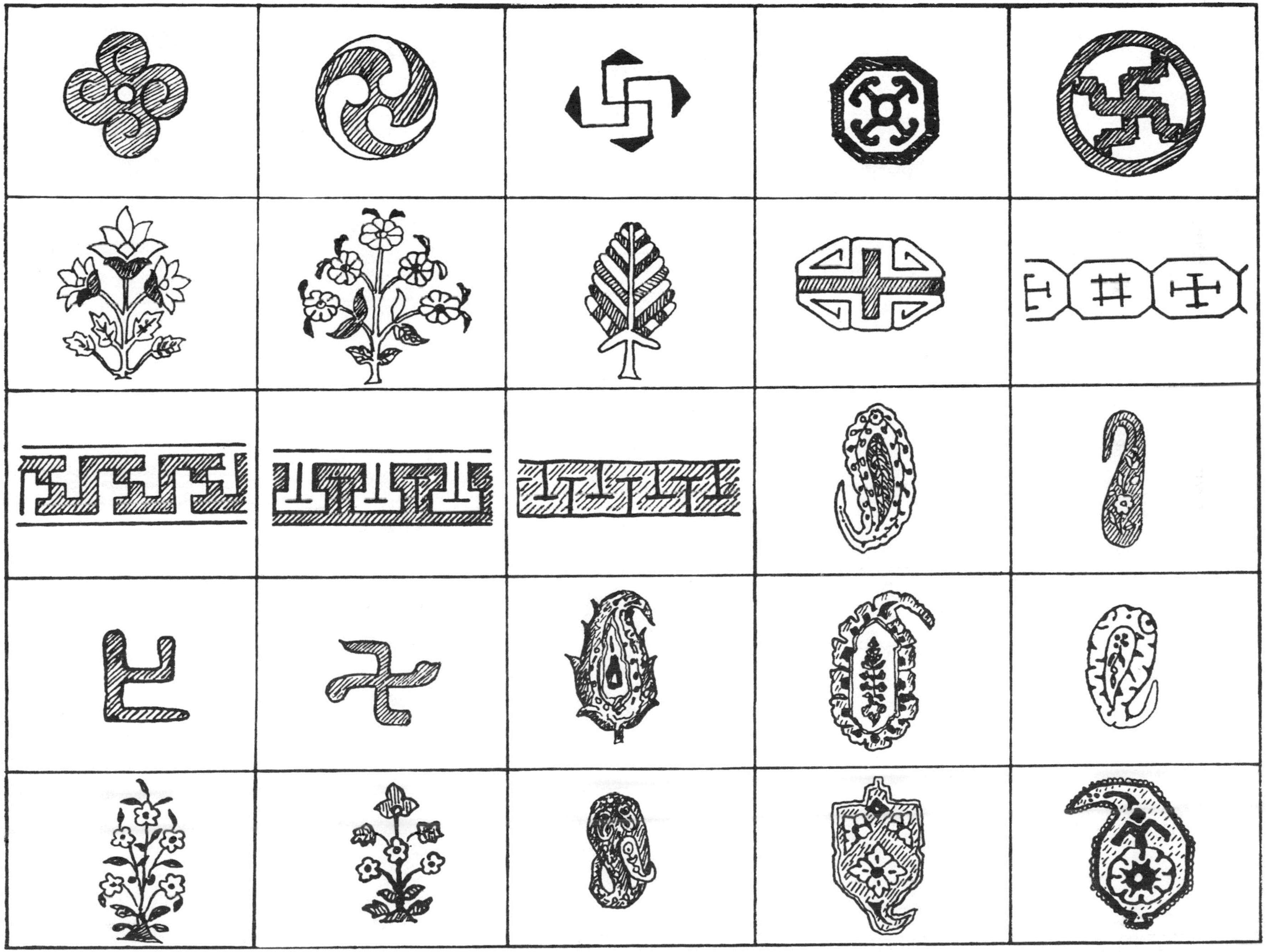

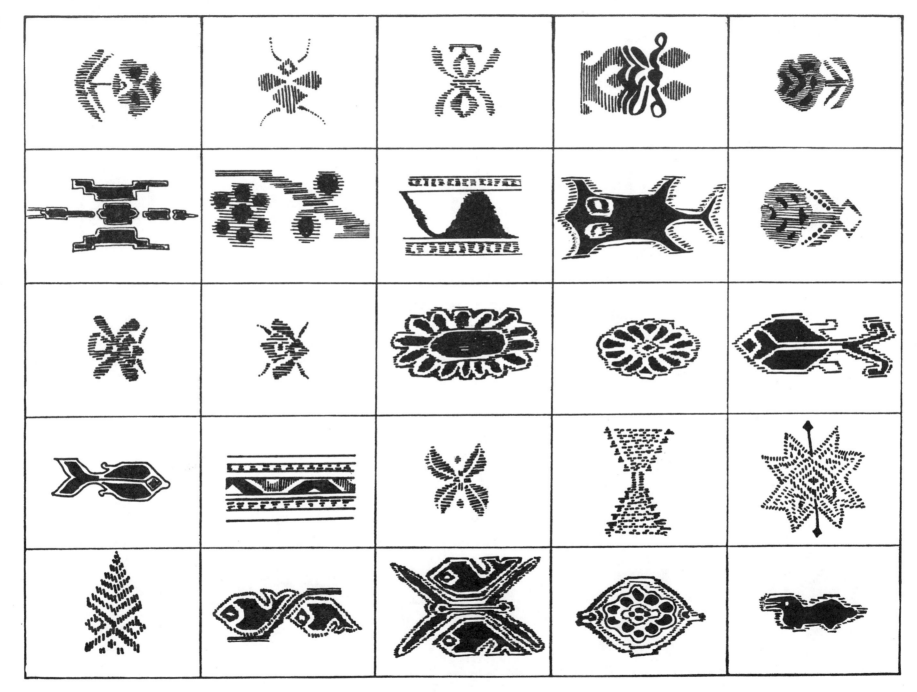

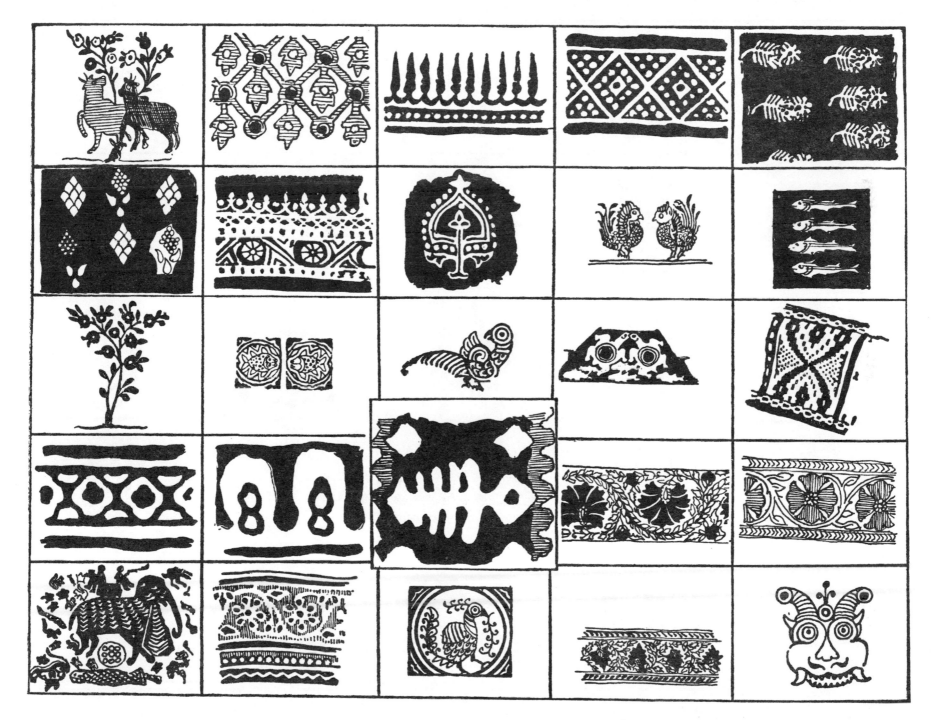

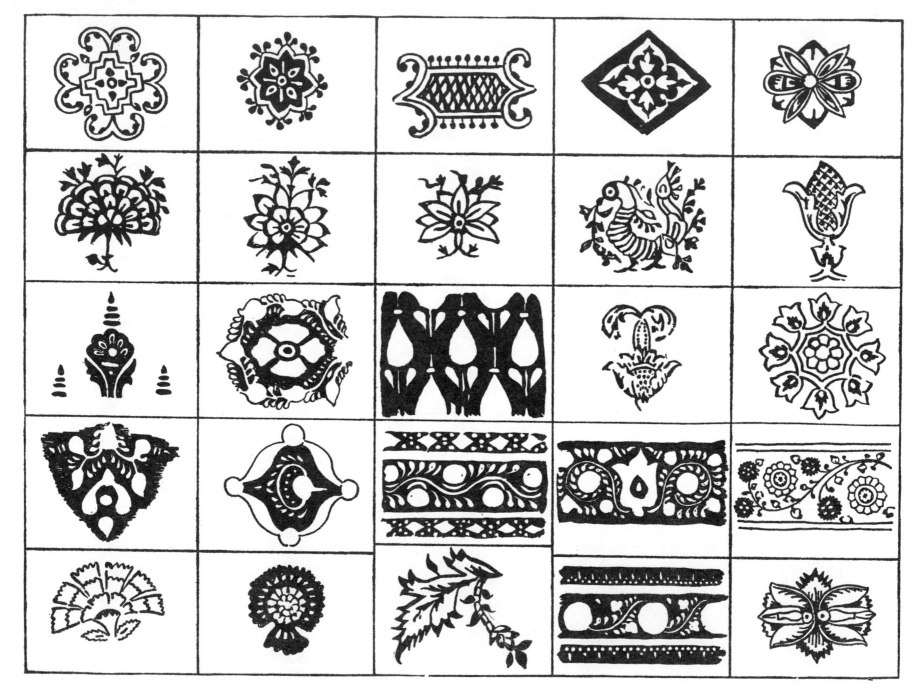

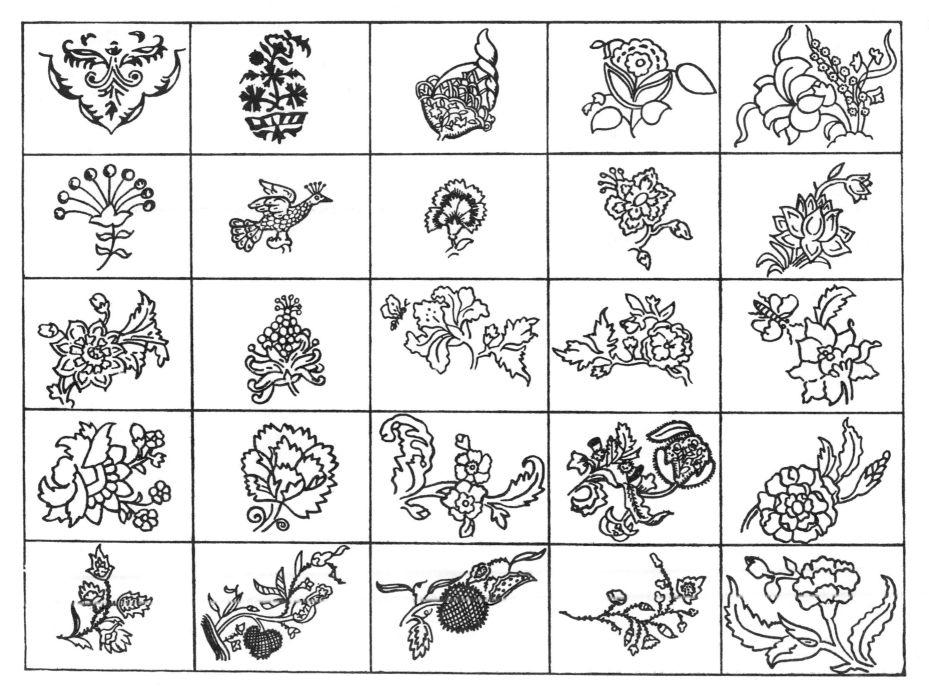

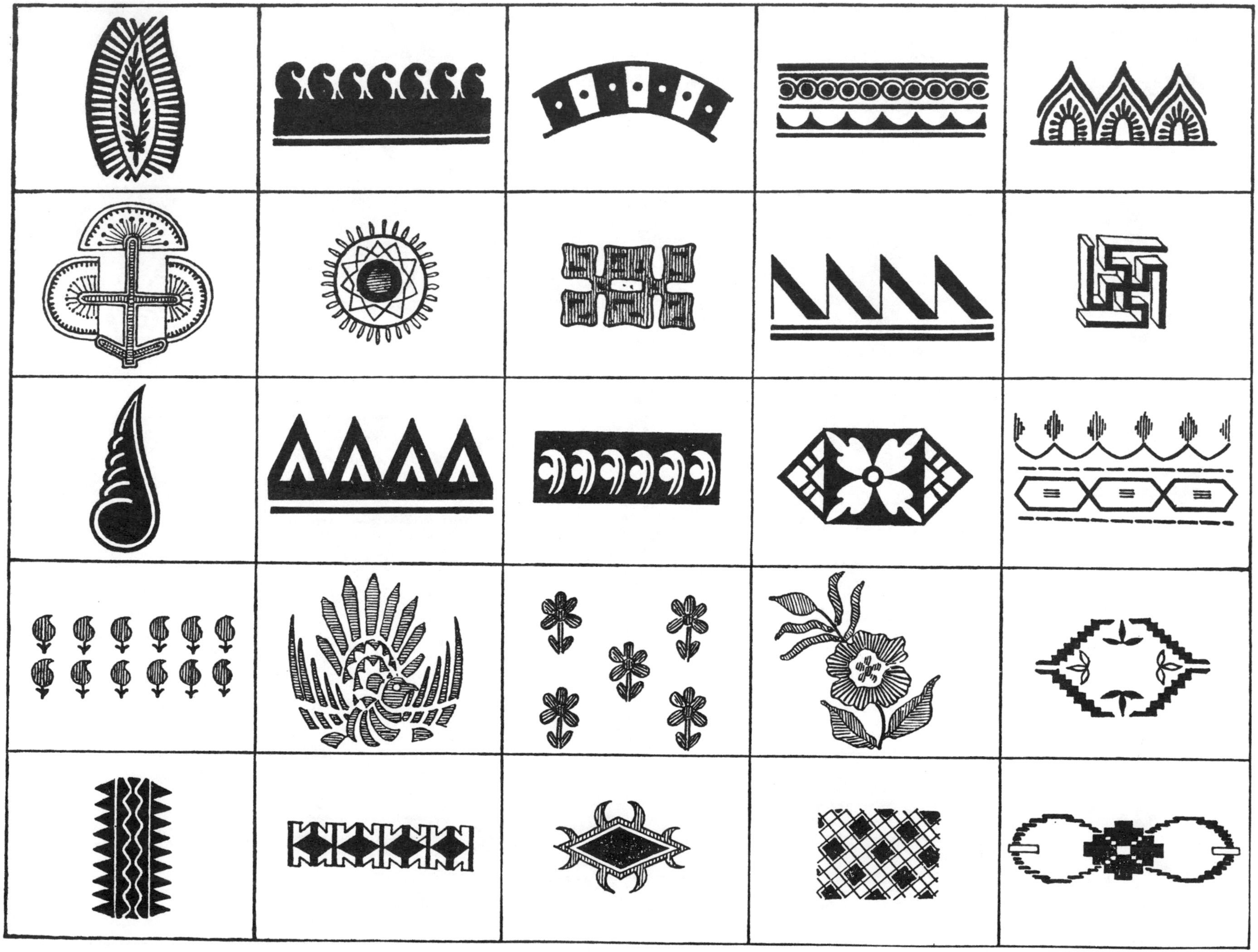

148

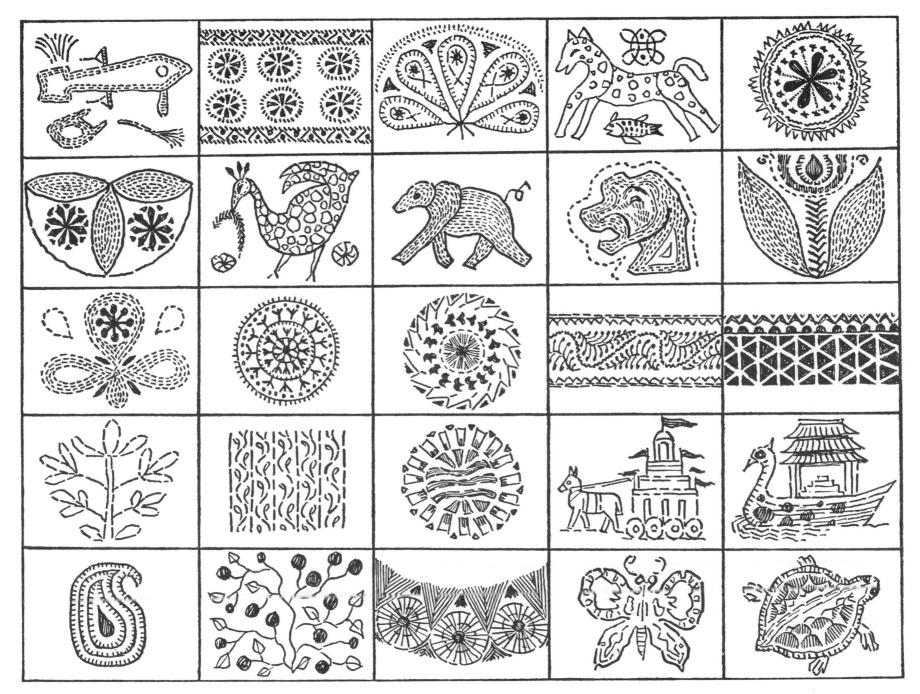

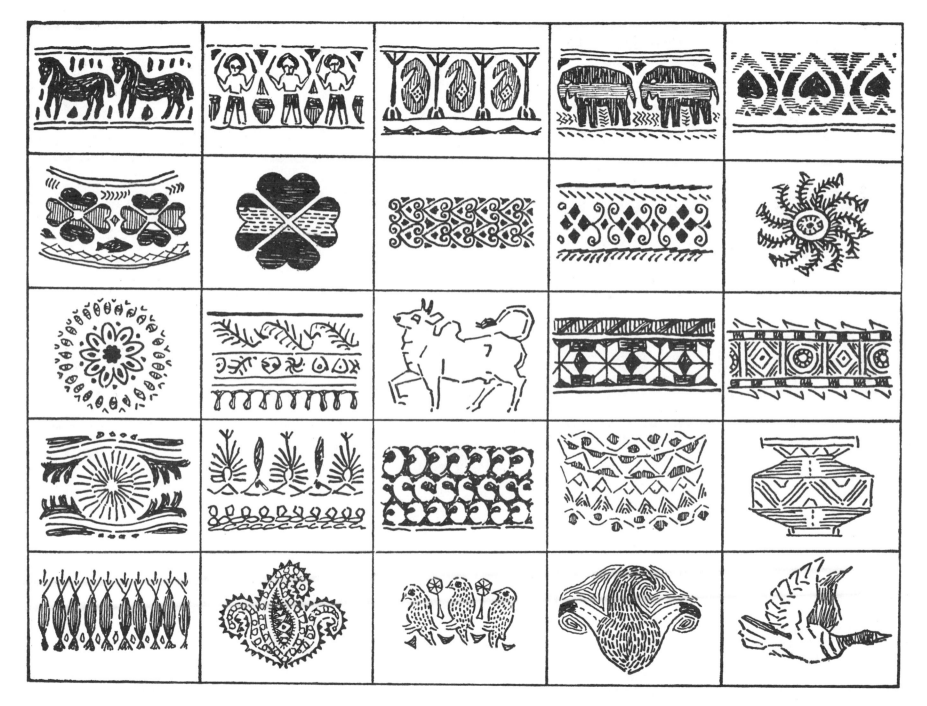

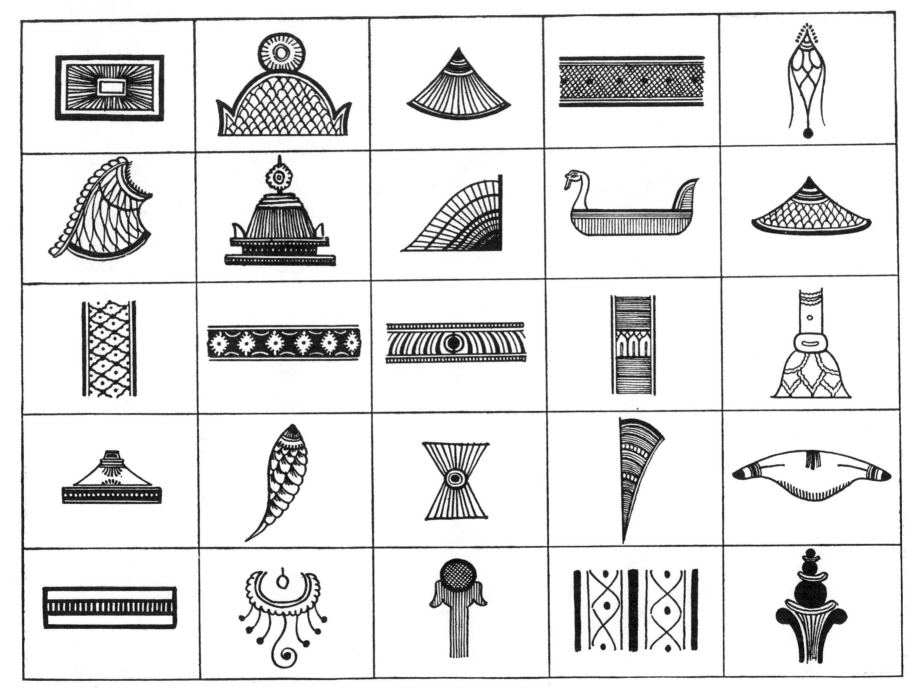

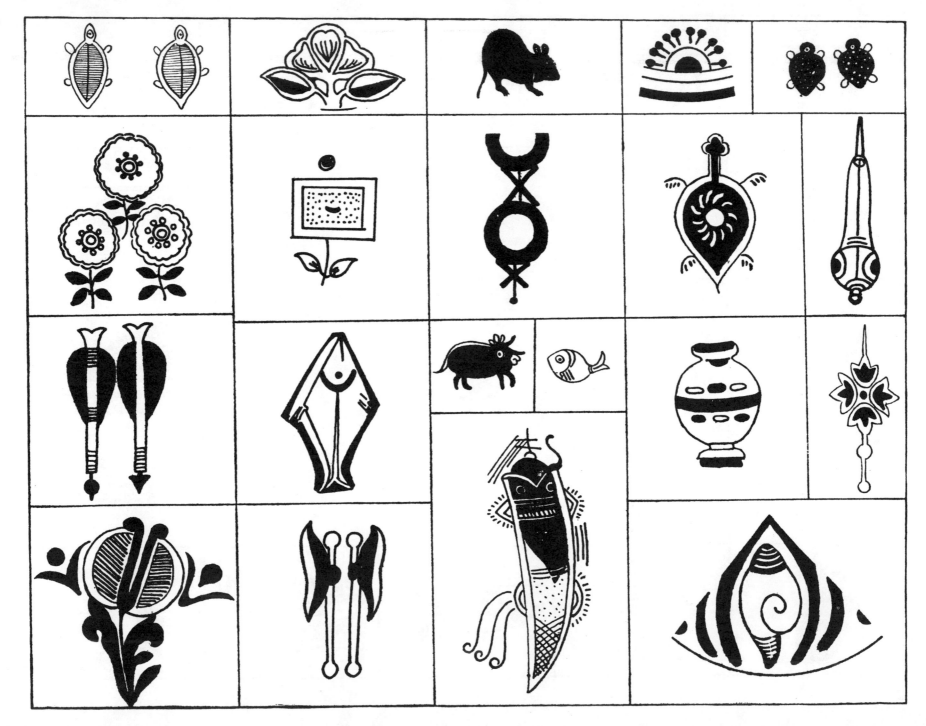

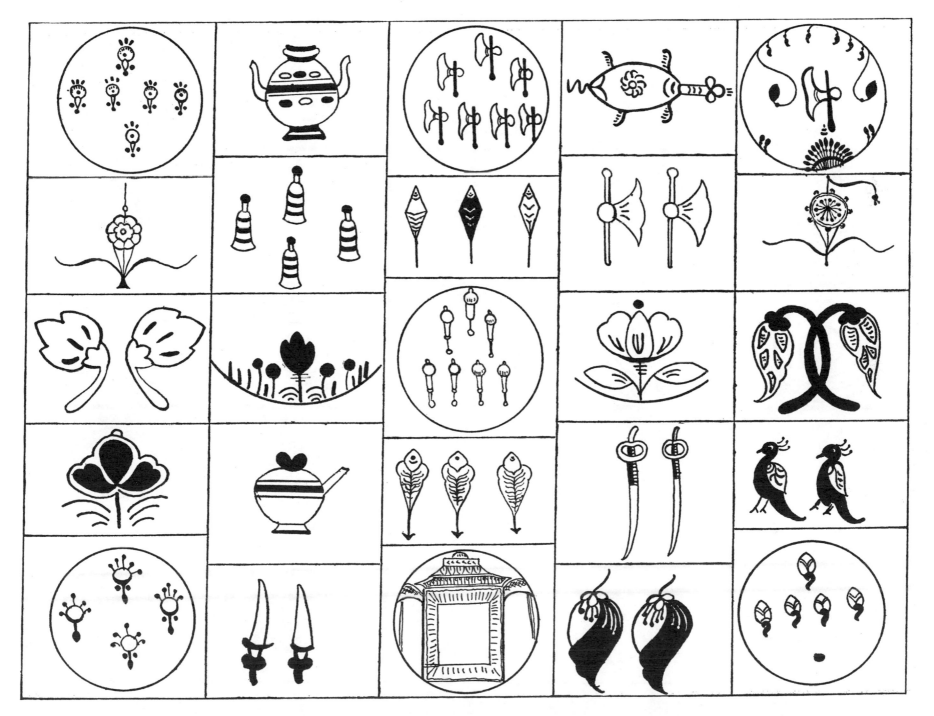

157

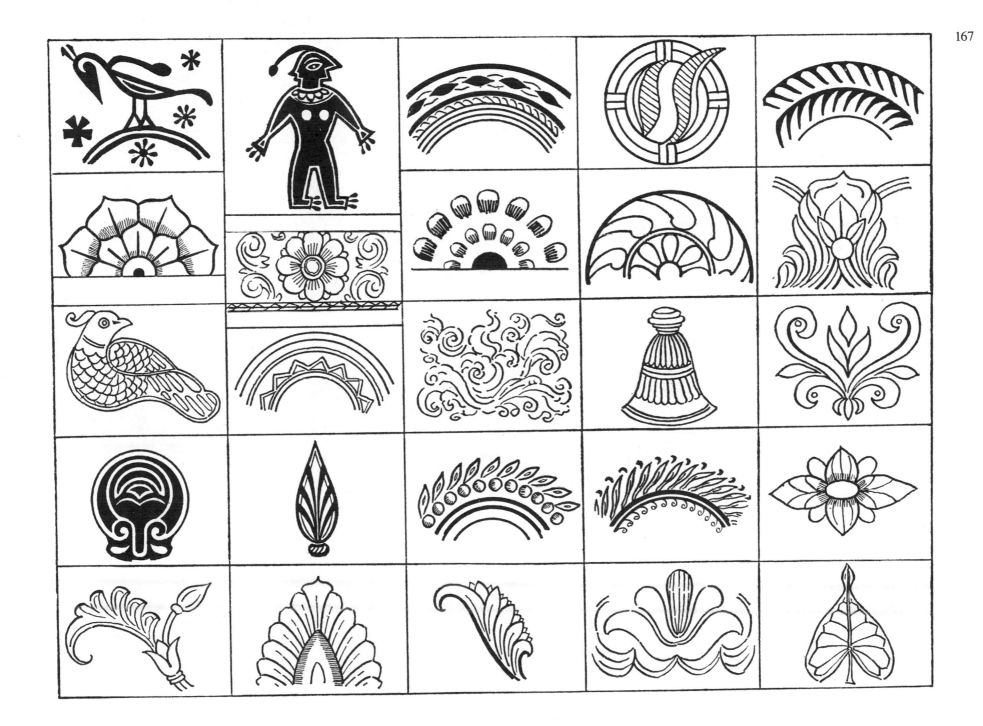

172

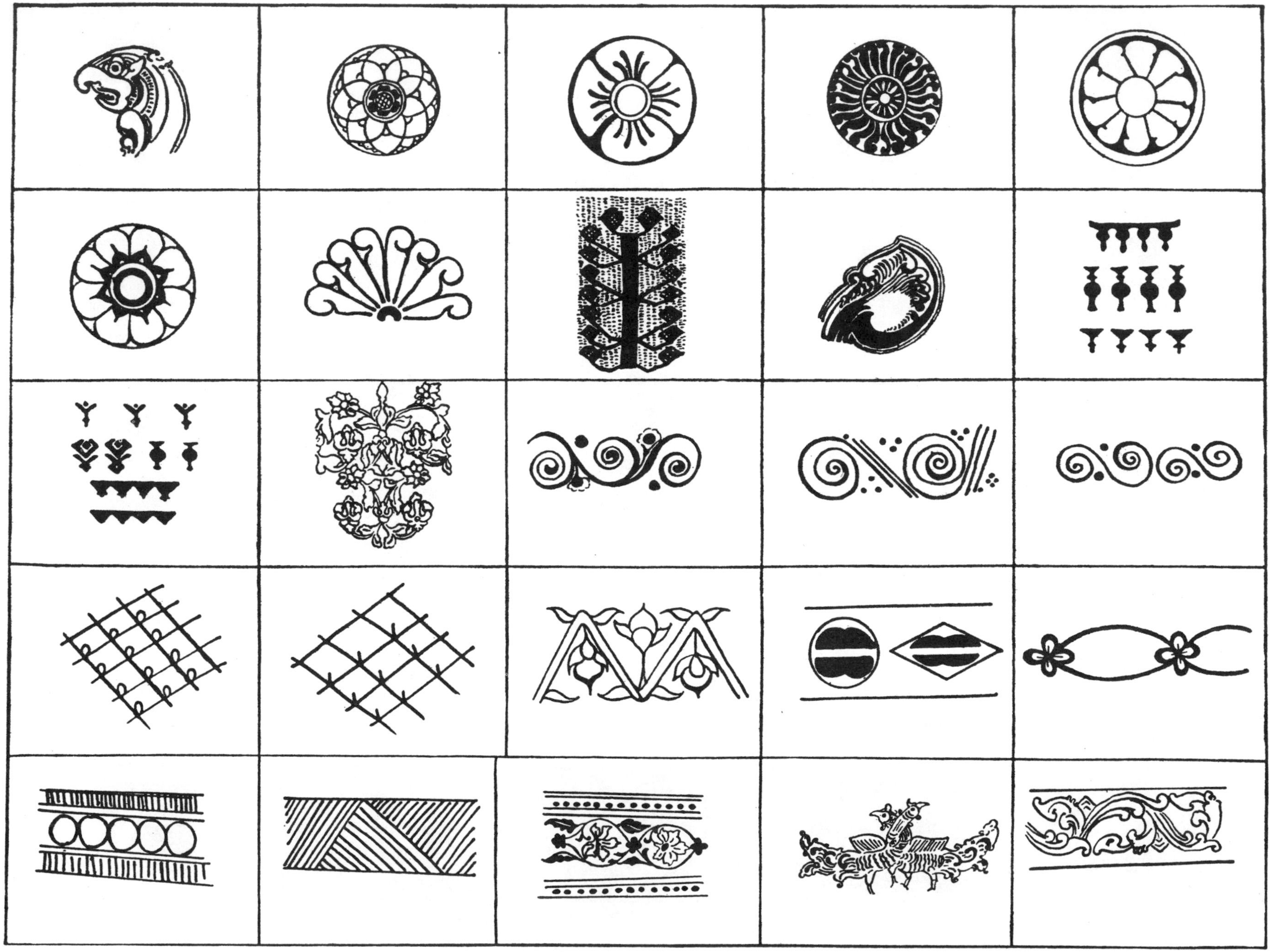

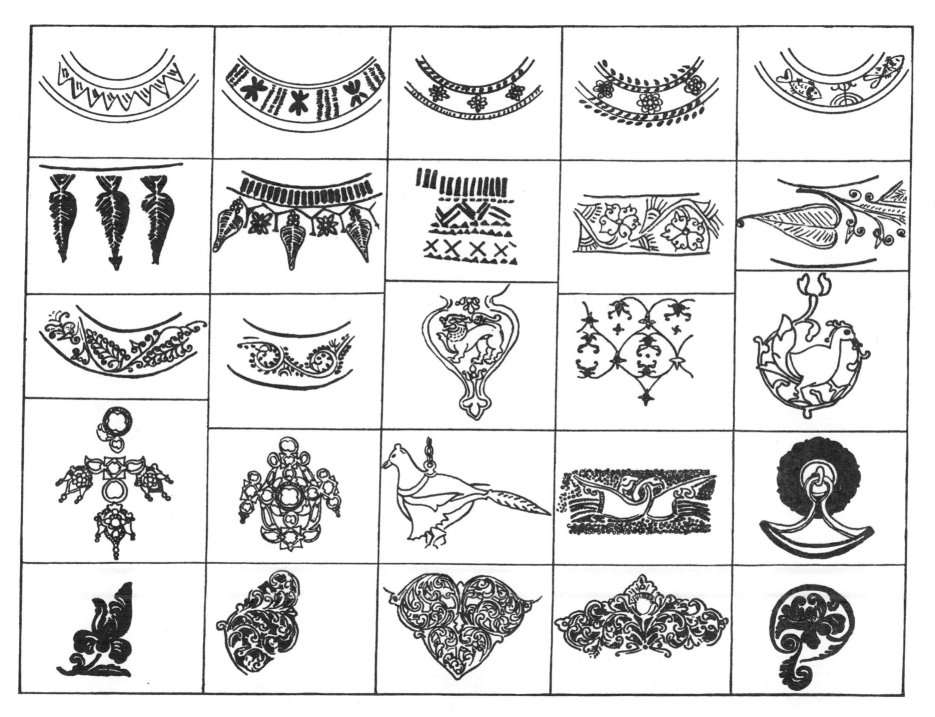

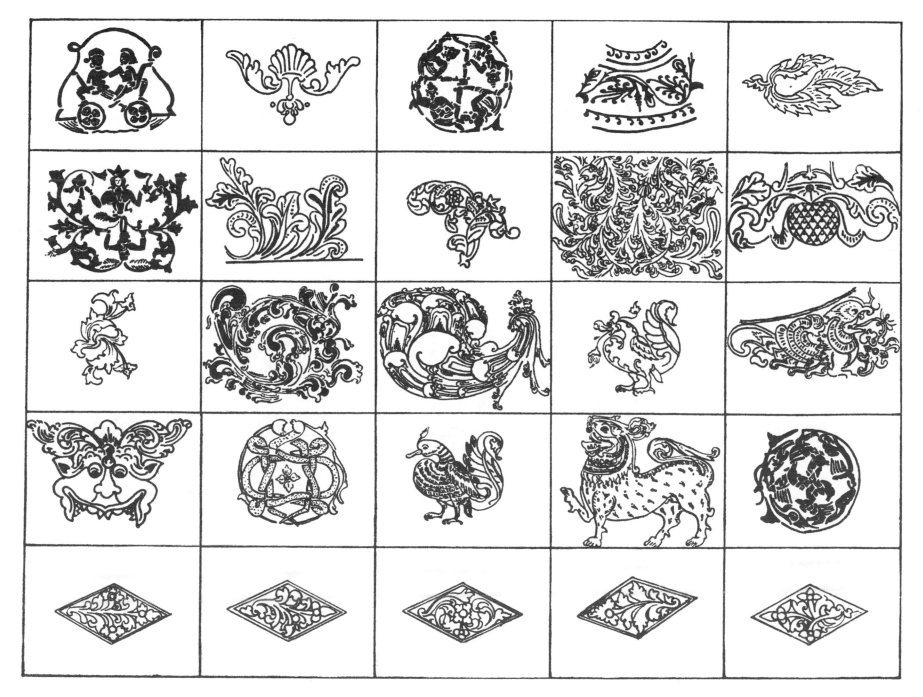

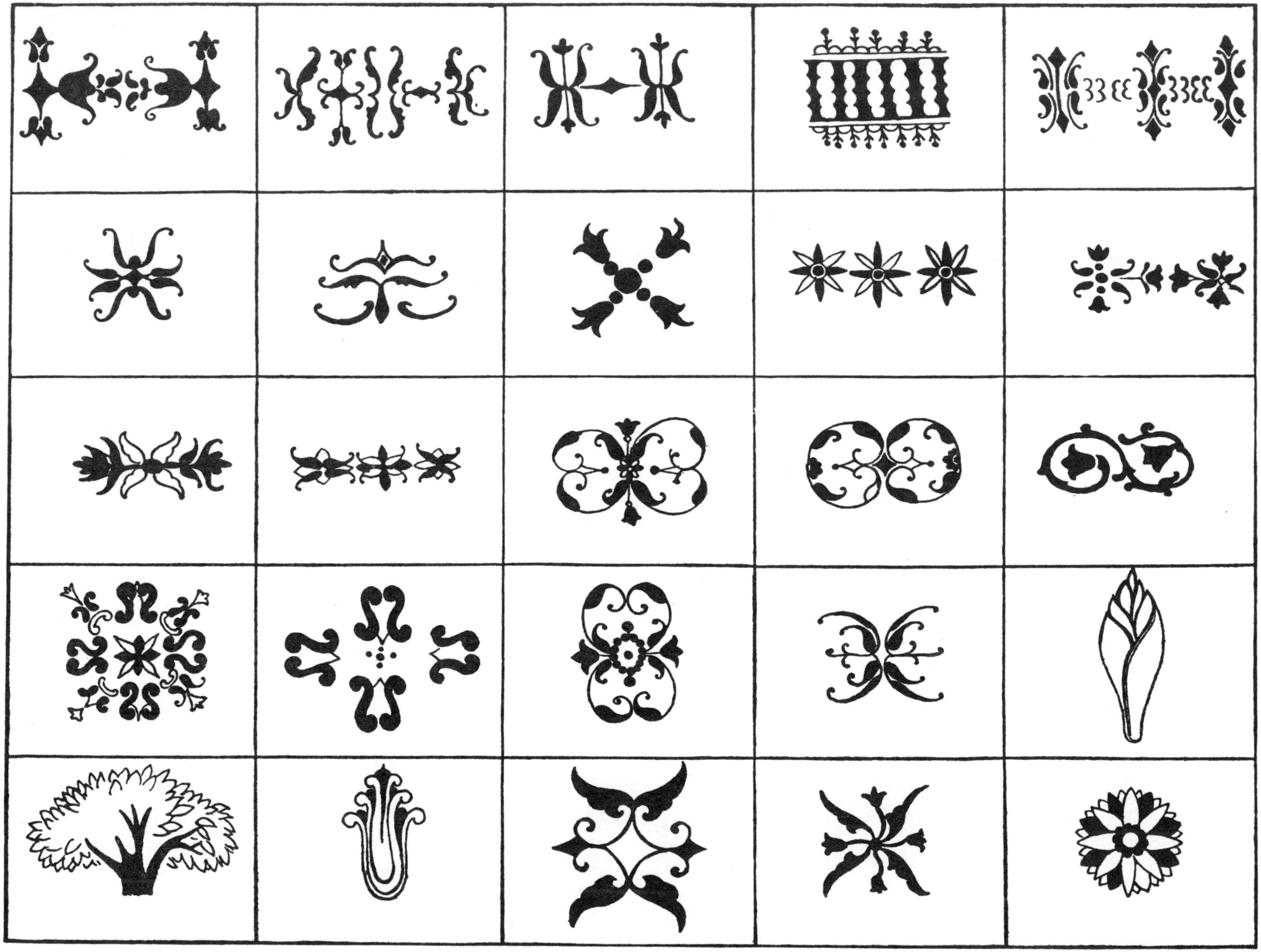

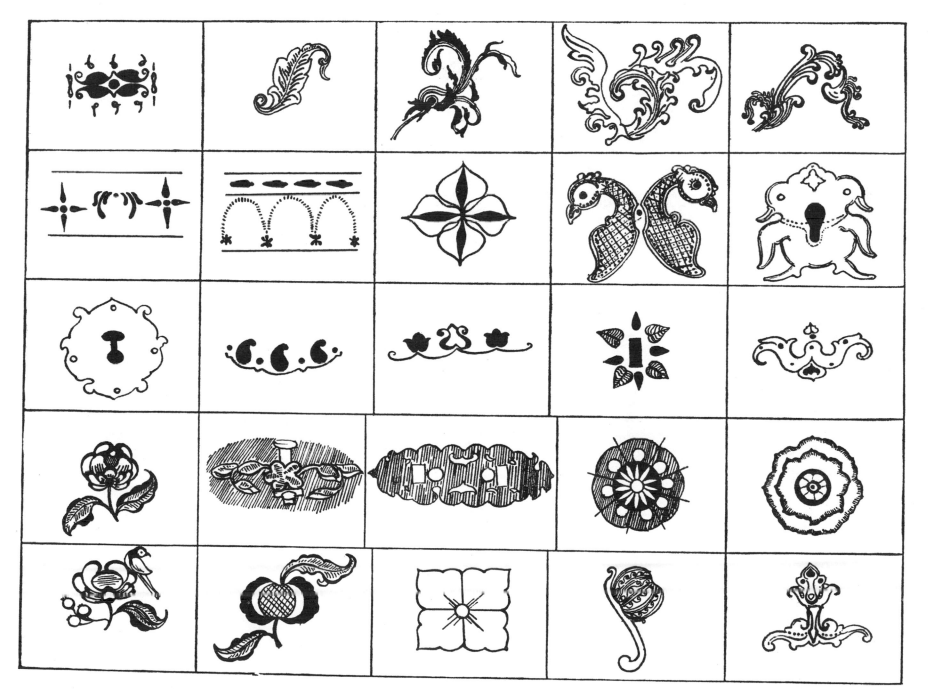

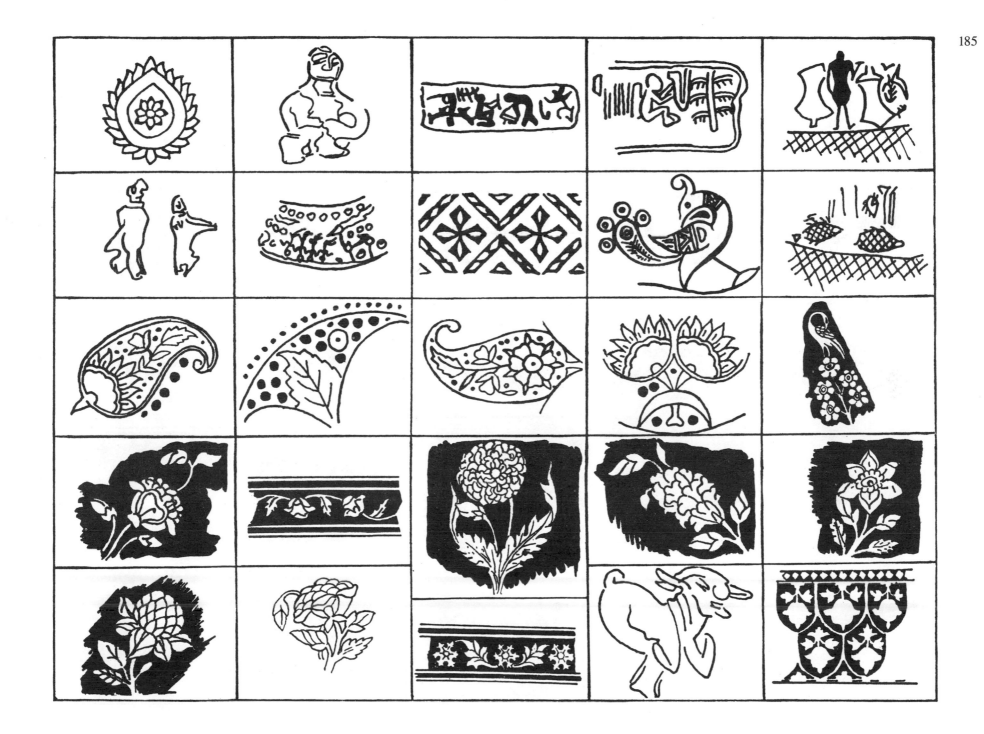

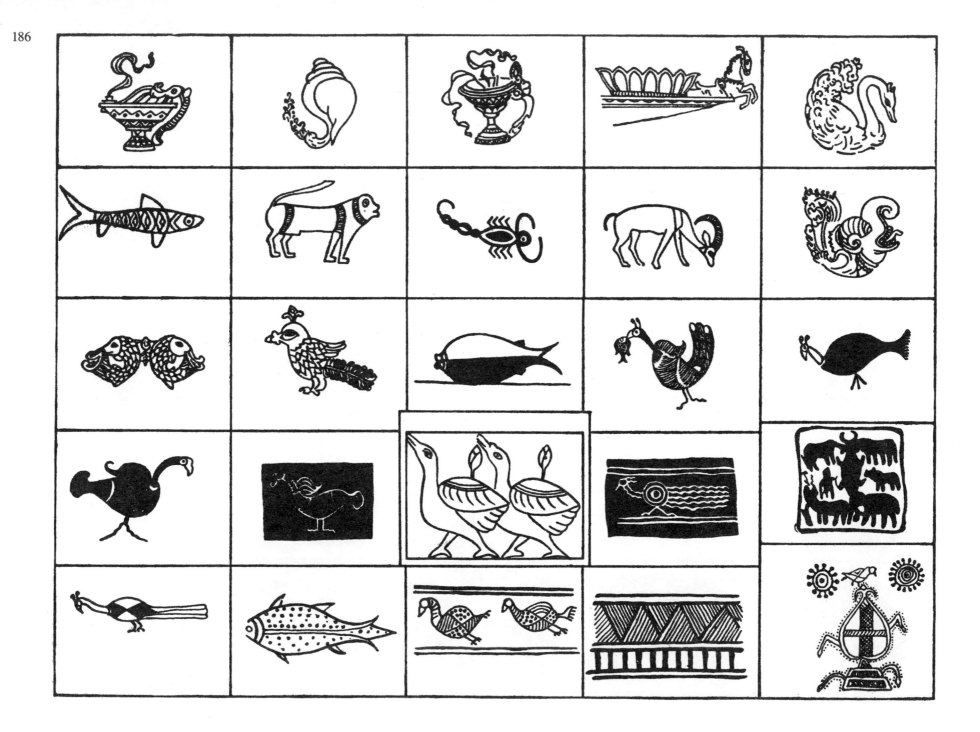

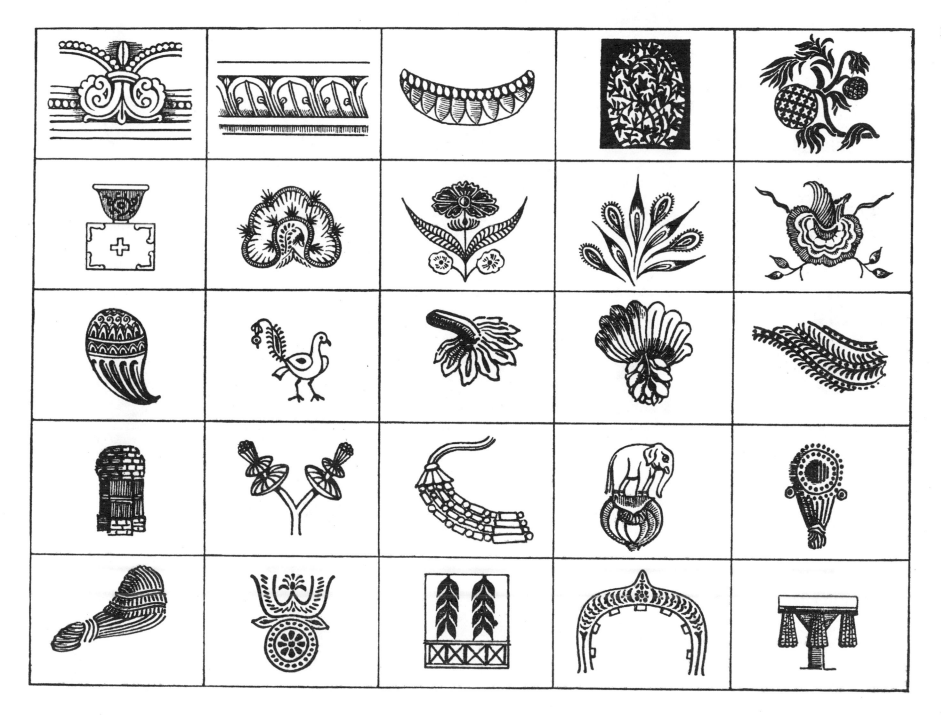

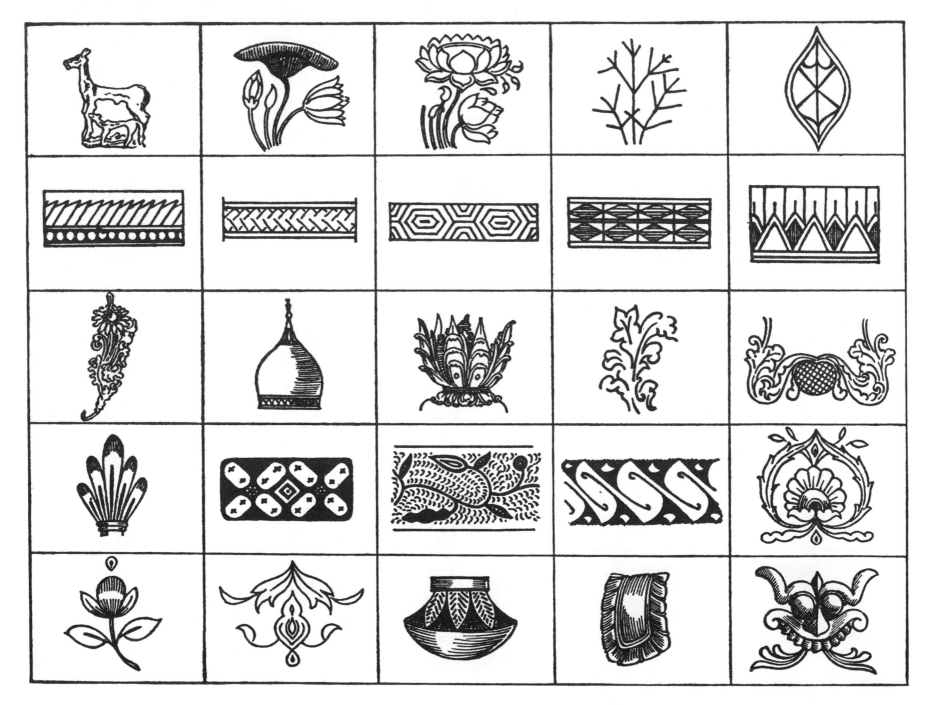

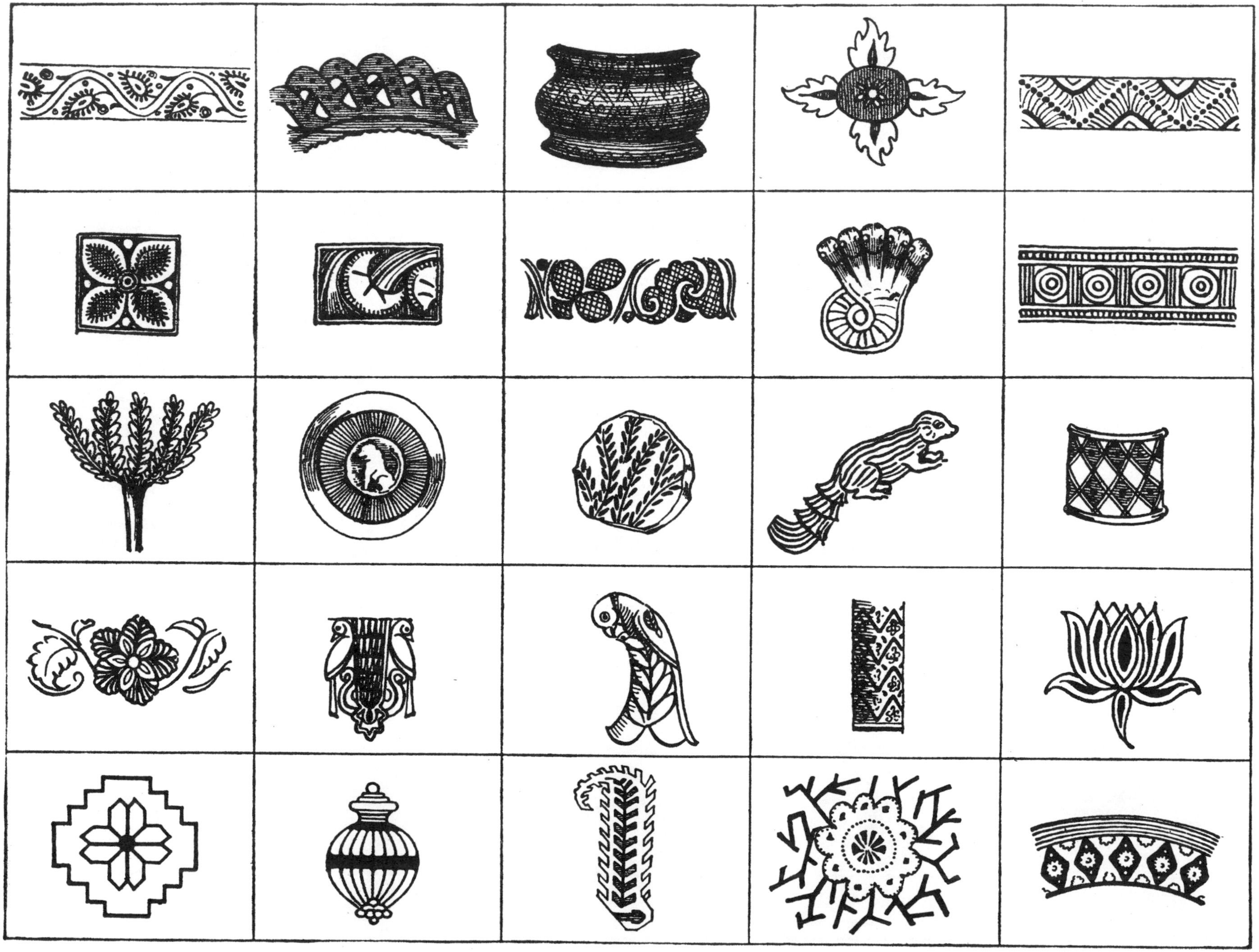

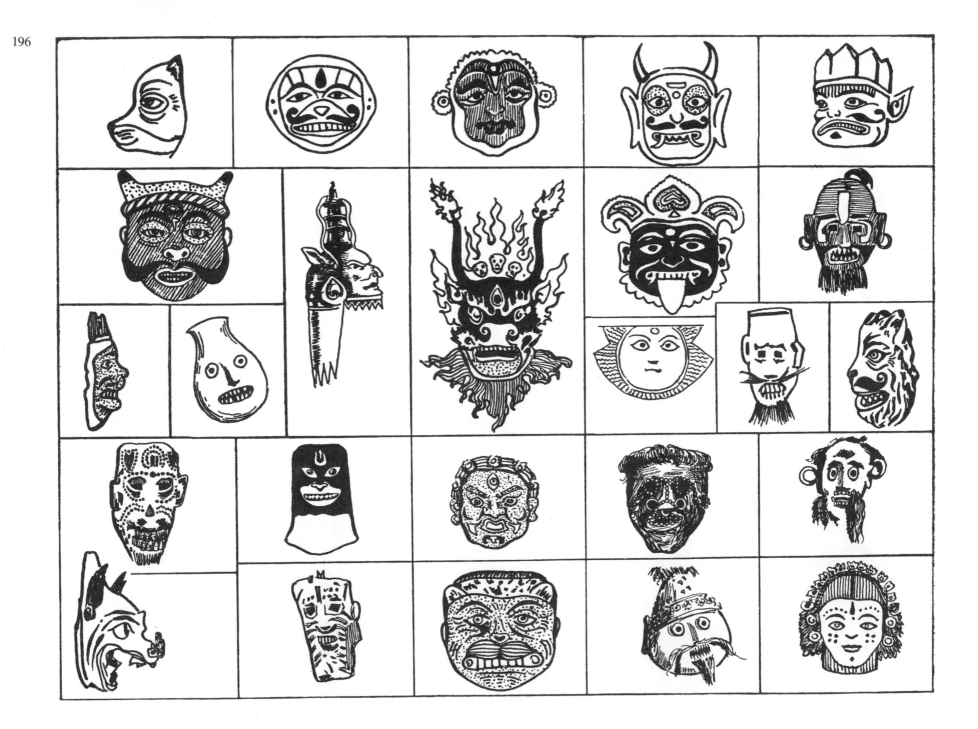

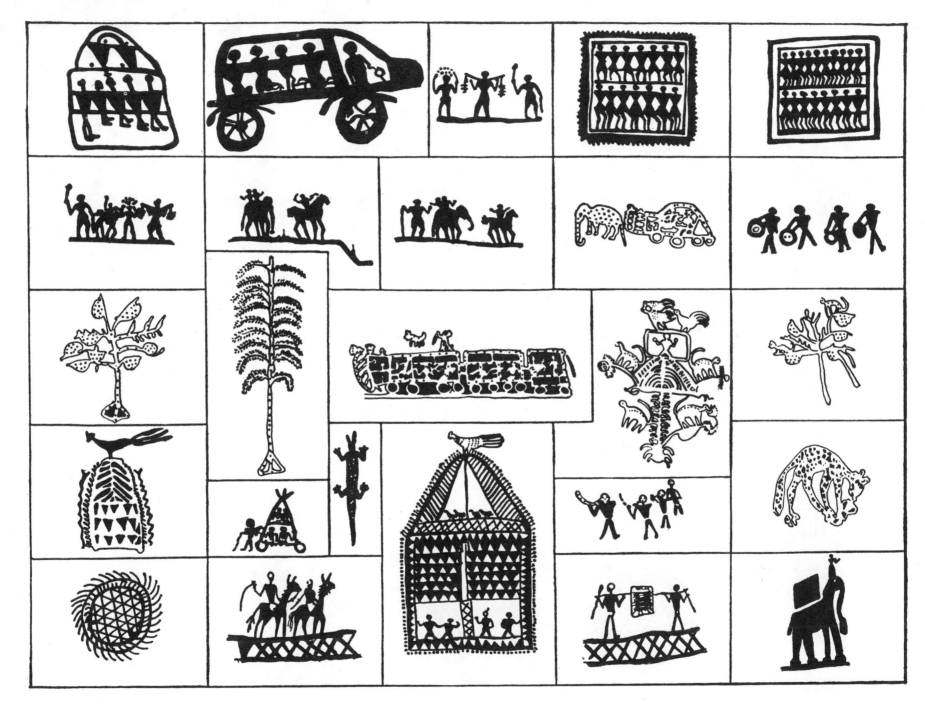

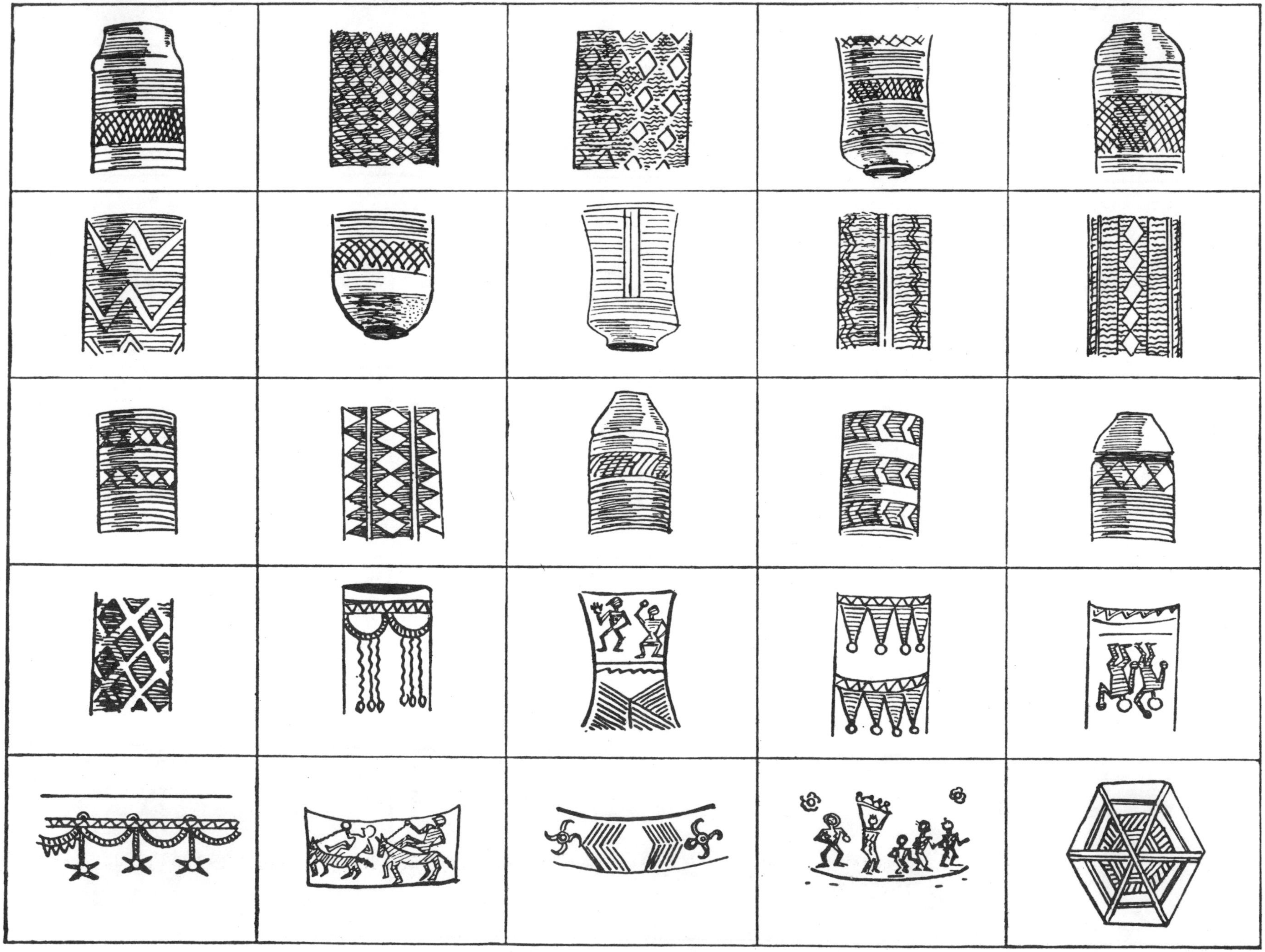